A Shattered Youth

A SHATTERED YOUTH

SURVIVING THE KHMER ROUGE

SATHAVY KIM

Every effort has been made to contact the copyright holders of material reproduced in this text. In cases where these efforts have been unsuccessful, the copyright holders are asked to contact the publishers directly.

First published in French in 2008 as *Jeunesse Brisée* by Actes Sud. This edition published in 2010 by Maverick House Publishers.

Maverick House Publishers, Office 19, Dunboyne Business Park, Dunboyne, Co. Meath, Ireland.
info@maverickhouse.com
http://www.maverickhouse.com

ISBN: 978-1-905379-70-5

French language © Sathavy Kim/Actes Sud, 2008.
English language translation copyright © Mary Byrne, 2010.

The publisher acknowledges the financial assistance of Ireland Literature Exchange (translation fund), Dublin, Ireland.
www.irelandliterature.com
info@irelandliterature.com

The paper used in this book comes from wood pulp of managed forests. For every tree felled, at least one tree is planted, thereby renewing natural resources.

A CIP catalogue record for this book is available from the British Library and the Irish Copyright libraries.

CONTENTS

ACKNOWLEDGEMENTS

Shattered Youth is the result of a labour that has been buried within me for almost thirty years. Digging it up was made possible by the encouragement of my close friends and relatives.

My first thoughts are for Vanny, *korngchalat* survivor, for her friendly and constant availability to talk with me about our memories. Without my fortuitous meeting with her in 2000, this story would have remained a family document only.

My thanks also go to Marie, my colleague and faithful friend, who, eleven years ago, encouraged me to make my first pilgrimage to Phum Thmey. That visit allowed me to resume contact with the villagers of Phum Thmey, and by means of dialogue, to rediscover the traces of my youth.

My gratitude and affection also go to Ta Chourp and Yeay Pheap, who took me in, to their children, and to the villagers of Phum Thmey. I owe them all my life; they supported me and warmed my heart during those four black years without my family.

I wish to express my gratitude to the Cambodian Documentation Centre, which gave me access to the archived documents from this period and allowed me to reproduce them.

I especially thank my husband Borng Do, for his affection, advice, and constant support. This book wouldn't have seen the light of day without his constant presence. I wrote *A Shattered Youth* by projecting myself into his eyes: putting his soul beside mine made writing this personal narrative easier.

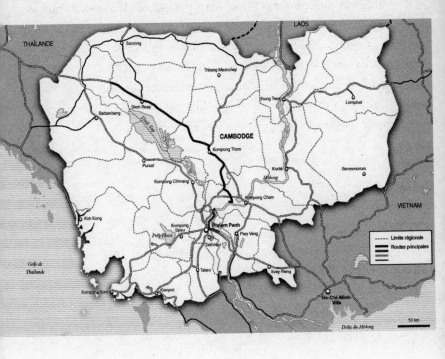

Victory breeds hatred
The defeated live in pain
The peaceful live happily
Giving up both victory and defeat.
Buddha, *Dhammapada*, "Sukha Vagga"

My name is Sathavy and I am the eldest of seven children. My father was a teacher but his real passion was for the land, and from the time I was small he taught me how to grow rice and traditional crops, such as salad and tomatoes.

Ours was a very united family, and both my parents were hard workers. They wanted to make sure my siblings and I would one day go to college, in spite of our provincial isolation. My mother was a seamstress and worked ceaselessly because she couldn't bear the idea of any of us ever being in need. I spent much of my childhood watching her work, and from an early age it was clear to me that she dreamed of a better life for my sisters and me. So, to prepare me for an improved city life, I was sent to secondary school in Battambang, the second largest town in the kingdom, and then on to Phnom Penh, Cambodia's capital city.

In 1975 the Khmer Rouge, led by Pol Pot, took control of Phnom Penh by force and my family and I, along with every other citizen of the city, were forced to evacuate. What followed was four years of genocide and unimaginable horror, which left over 1.7 million of my people dead. Although we were undoubtedly relieved when the Khmer Rouge were overthrown in 1979, during the ten years of Vietnamese occupation that followed, we continued to live in constant fear of being suspected of treason. Danger was still all around us, and the countryside was riddled with Khmer Rouge soldiers trying to regain control of the country. But no matter how much the threat of danger remained, it was still more bearable than the four years of oppression and genocide we had just lived through. It was as if the Khmer Rouge had completely desensitised us, and we no longer recognised how appalling our circumstances still were.

In 1997 Hun Sen, leader of the Cambodian People's Party, overthrew Prime Minister Norodom Ranariddh in a bloody coup. I was forced to live through the same scenes all over again: smoke in the sky, panic in the streets, people fleeing their homes with only a small bundle over their shoulders. I began to have vivid nightmares, and night after night they invaded my sleep: the bloody arbitrariness of the Khmer Rouge regime; being brutally awoken at three in the morning to go to work; the fear of going down into the water in the paddy fields; being hungry and exhausted; being scared they would take me away; seeing soldiers take other people away with their hands tied behind their backs.

I had been working as a judge for almost fifteen years, when, in 1997, I was given an opportunity to spend a year working and studying at a law school in The University of Michigan in the United States. The coup took place just a couple of days before I was due to leave and the administration where I worked had doubts about letting me go. They were afraid that if I left I wouldn't come back, but I decided the opportunity was too good to miss, and I was glad of the chance to distance myself from the country. My family was happy to let me go; an important lesson we had learned from the Khmer Rouge regime was that it was better to be separate than to stay together in one place; if something happened, at least some of us would be safe.

Two months after my arrival in Michigan, however, I still couldn't sleep at night and continued to have nightmares. At the law school, I was asked to give a presentation on the post-conflict situation in Cambodia after the withdrawal of the Khmer Rouge. I was so moved to tears during the presentation that I lost my voice. It took me a long time to regain my composure after that and for months afterwards I felt unsettled.

I was very fortunate, however, to have a job which gave me opportunities to meet people from non-governmental and humanitarian organisations. I found I liked being around others and I sometimes told parts of my story to friends and acquaintances. In my family too, we often referred to our daily life under the Pol Pot regime. Talking about the past in this way convinced me that things had really changed, but it still wasn't enough to free me of my nightmares; they continued to rise to the top of my mind, like fermenting bubbles in a glass of beer.

Some of my friends encouraged me to write about my past, but I was so damaged by everything that had happened that for a long time I couldn't bear to deliberately relive those experiences. I'd spent 20 years trying to evade my past, but I began to realise that there was a void in my life and I needed to fill it. I knew that if I was ever to move on I would have to make a break with those close friends who were now long dead, but continued to haunt me. I began by filling in the blanks in the history of my family, and in doing so I was able to recollect my stolen life.

With the support and encouragement of my husband Borng Do, I went back to the places where I had been held. I made several trips to the village of Phum Thmey to see the family who'd been my safe haven under the Khmer Rouge regime, and I even met the leaders and members of the labour camp where I was forced to work. I visited places that still bear the scars of the atrocities committed there, and by naming them I hope to help heal the wounds that still remain.

My story is a genuine personal account, and one that could have been told by thousands of other women who are no longer here to tell it for themselves. My intention, therefore, in writing this book was to move beyond the idea of a personal chronicle. Instead of merely documenting my own life, I wanted to document the daily reality experienced by so many women during those three years, eight months and twenty days we lived under the Khmer Rouge regime. I spent most of that time in the *korngchalat*, a forced-labour camp in Kampong Cham, the province most completely permeated by the influence of the Khmer Rouge.

Working in the labour camp became our domestic reality, and we spent each day in submission. We were forced to work as prisoners, and to search each day for water and food. We were obliged to sit through criticism sessions each evening, and every minute of our lives was spent in the repression of our identities, our religious traditions, and all our cultural references.

In our daily life in this open air prison, the aspirations of the Angkar, the political organisation behind the Khmer Rouge, began to appear little by little. Although a distant and removed institution, the *korngchalat* acted as a constant reinforcement of the most radical of the Angkar's philosophies and procedures, and went completely against everything human dignity demanded. Later we learned that the final objective of the Angkar was to create a "New" being, one who was totally subject to the concentration-camp system and possessed no sense of individuality.

My personal journey is, therefore, also a social chronicle and a testimony to the substance of Khmer women, who, to their great honour, managed to retain their humanity even throughout those dark years. This book is a homage to the great majority of them, who courageously defended their dignity, even to the death. It is also a homage to those female survivors who, after the fall of Pol Pot and his regime, were the first to give back meaning to our existence by rebuilding the family unit, and weaving a social network around our national identity.

This book is organised according to the rhythms of the universe of female *korngchalat* workers, furnishing their labour to the Angkar without limit, and often without purpose. It is also punctuated by chronological stages in the concentration-camp system until it collapsed in early 1979. A glossary completes this account, with a translation of all the words in the Khmer language which were used frequently during that period, and their specific meaning inside the system to which we were subjected. The Khmer language, which is rich in ancient sources such as Pali and Sanskrit, is a language of refined subtleties, of tales and legends. But it had become an instrument of combat. To support the domination to which we were subjected, each word was carefully weighed up to best measure the gravity of an order or situation. I felt it was useful to give this permanent linguistic reference, not only as an indication of the violence of the words themselves under Khmer Rouge ideology, but also to highlight the Khmer language of today, which still carries its traditions within it—as well as the red brand of violence.

This is the story of how I, and Cambodia's women, struggled to survive under the Khmer Rouge.

PART I

NEW PEOPLE

CHAPTER 1

Return to the Light

The law of the eight principles:
Be able to remain silent
Know if it's better to eat or to refrain
Be able to keep on going, although the place be pleasant
Be hungry but know how to refrain
Be weary but manage to stay awake
Be able to describe exactly what you have seen
Be able to hold what you must hold
Do not eat the whole

Cambodian code of 1898

On 20 December 1978 in Reay Pay, a village in the province of Kampong Cham, a rumour went around our camp—the *korngchalat*—that a battle was raging between Khmer Rouge soldiers and Vietnamese troops along the Cambodian-Vietnam border.

The *korngchalat* had been my world since I was 21 years old in 1975, when the Khmer Rouge had marched through Phnom Penh and forced me from my home.

The Khmer cadres now referred increasingly to our Vietnamese neighbours as enemies of the Khmer people, and we could see that the leaders of the camp at all levels were demoralised. They stopped supervising us, and during the first days of January 1979 they began to disappear, one after another.

Around 8 p.m. on 5 or 6 January, I heard the sound of tanks in the distance. A little later the clanking of tracked vehicles approached, and several tanks and trucks came into view near our camp. I was ready to drop from exhaustion, but I gathered whatever provisions I could—some rice, beans and dried fish from the communal kitchen—and hoped to flee before the troops confronted us. The food stores, which had always been forbidden to us, were now accessible, but we had no means of transport by which to leave, and we weren't sure whether it was safe for us on the roads. We hesitated, not knowing what to do.

Later that night, we heard more sounds of fighting nearby. No one could sleep, and by now most people were ready to take their chances on the road. Some took chickens, pigs, cows, and buffalo from the village's *sahakor*, a cooperative set up by the Angkar to distribute food and direct labour. Others even went so far as to hitch up a cart. As for the rest of us, we didn't dare budge. We were traumatised, still obeying the Angkar. We feared there would be retribution for the raids on the sahakor if the camp leaders were to return. I waited on with a few friends, other members of the *korngchalat* but after several hours, when no one returned, and no orders were forthcoming, we decided to leave too.

After four years of being told when I could sleep, eat, work and move, I had no idea where I was headed, and wondered whether I should go to the neighbouring village of Phum Thmey, or back to my family in Siem Reap. For almost four years I had had no news of my family. I felt like I was floating on an ocean with no idea where the shore was. I had no real family ties in Phum Thmey, but it was where the Angkar had originally placed me, and where I had the only family I now knew.

The girls who were with me were happy and radiant for the first time in years, like birds flying the coop. We walked together quickly, each hoping beyond hope to find our loved ones safe and well. We had no idea what was happening back in the village, and on the main roads we met truck after truck of Vietnamese soldiers. We hid our heads in our *krama*, a multipurpose scarf worn by both men and women, and dared not look at the soldiers. The Vietnamese soldiers were both invader and liberator, and we had mixed feelings about them. They had just freed us from the Khmer Rouge for which we were extremely grateful, but we were afraid of all soldiers and had been told the Vietnamese raped and beat women. We hurried past them as quickly as we could and kept our heads down.

Tanks came and went along all the roads, and both the Vietnamese and the Khmer troops called out to us as they passed: "Everyone has to go back to where they came from, because the war is finished and the country is free".

Did that word still have any meaning? It sounded strange and foreign to us. On 17 April 1975, the Khmer Rouge had also said the country was free; we didn't know what to believe anymore. After two days' walking, we arrived in Peam Chikorng, where the roads to several villages meet. We were still convinced the Khmer Rouge were hiding somewhere and would soon return.

People said it was the end of Democratic Kampuchea, the name the Khmer Rouge had ascribed to our country, but I wondered whether this was fact or fiction. Everywhere I looked, I saw people fleeing in utter disarray. Thousands fled to Thailand with the Khmer Rouge, most of them at gunpoint. Those who remained took the food supplies of the Khmer Rouge cooperatives and ate their fill for the first time in years. With no thought for the future, they killed pigs, cattle, and buffalo. They then took kitchen utensils, farm tools, and the remaining cattle, and took to the roads.

We were emerging from a night that had lasted for years, blinking as we stepped into the light. We still couldn't grasp the fact that our nightmare was over.

Like a free bird I gasped in the air. I was hungry, and for the first time in years, I ate a lot of rice as I needed. The only thing on my mind was to go back to my family in Siemreap. I was very tired, because I had a fever a couple days before, the Vietnamese came to liberate us.

Before the Khmer Rouge came to power, I was just a young student, an ordinary Cambodian, far removed from political movements which went unnoticed in my province of Battambang. I did remember the rise of the revolutionary dream, however; a dream incarnated by the Khmer Rouge, a dream of a new Cambodia. People talked of the Khmer issarak, or "Free Khmer"; these were splinter groups of which there were many in Phnom Penh. At the end of the 1960s only the issarak right-wing militants had survived, under the name Khmer sérei. They were opposed to the head of state Norodom Sihanouk up to his exile to China in 1970, when the prime minister, General Lon Nol, had orchestrated a coup against him.

I had also heard of a group termed the "Khmer Kraham" who claimed a doctrine of freedom and adopted the phrase "*Khmer romdoh*" or "liberated Khmer" as their emblem. Their main influence was the progress of the Vietnamese communists against whom they modelled themselves. I'd often heard my parents using the name "Khmer Kraham, Khmer Rouge" since I'd been in secondary school. In fact, this was an invention of Norodom Sihanouk who coined the term in 1968 during the course of one of the long flowing speeches he liked to give. Although he was popular, it wasn't enough to help him avoid the coup orchestrated by Lon Nol. That was the *coup d'état* that facilitated the rise in force of the Khmer Rouge.

When Pol Pot, leader of the Khmer Rouge, came to power, he committed himself to the elimination of those in his party who failed to share his "nationalist-Maoist" style of communism, and those among the general population who supported any form of opposition, real or imagined. But this movement wasn't uniform, and was only confirmed after the country was divided into political zones. The different zones of Democratic Kampuchea didn't always follow the directives of the central authority with the same rigour or brutality; it depended on the zone chiefs and their individual personalities. The centre zone to which I was deported was initially controlled, along with the north zone, by Koy Thuon, a former teacher. It was relatively spared at first, but summary executions sped up after his elimination in 1977, and our situation became more and more treacherous.

After more than five years of civil war (1970 to 1975) between the Khmer Rouge communists and the government in place of Lon Nol, supported by the US, Pol Pot's Democratic Kampuchea planned to mobilise the whole Khmer population and build a communist society based on the notion of an "agrarian utopia".

Everybody was sad, life was already difficult, some parts of the country were occupied by the Khmer Rouge, the land occupied by the government became smaller and smaller.

The urban population, or "New people" as we came to be known, was estimated at more than one million, and we were forced to integrate the peasant population and serve as basic labour. We were sent to forced-labour camps called *korngchalat* which were run by cooperatives answering to the Angkar. The Angkar's orders were reinforced by the Khmer Rouge soldiers, and we were obliged, under threat of torture or execution, to forget our education, our experience and our abilities. This primitive model has been described by historians as "agrarian collectivism of the bureaucratic variety". Obviously I knew nothing of all that when I was hastened onto the road to deportation in 1975. And that is how, instead of utopia, we were plunged into horror.

CHAPTER 2

EN ROUTE TO A SHATTERED YOUTH

Ye monks, learn that all existence is pain:
birth is pain, old age is pain.
It is like death, like union with the unpleasant,
like the separation from that which we love,
like unsatisfied desire…
At the root of this universal pain is the desire for existence, the
sensual and intellectual hunger for pleasure — and even the
hunger for death.

Buddha, The Sermon at Benares

My parents wanted me to serve as an example for my six brothers and sisters, and my father often said that the first child has to choose the right direction so the others will follow. Until I was nine, however, I lived with my grandparents, not far from my parents' house. It was, and still is, common in Khmer families for grandparents to take an active role in bringing up their grandchildren, and my grandmother in particular loved children. She had had only three children herself (my mother being the youngest), but it is common in our tradition to have much larger families, and my grandparents, therefore, raised both my younger cousin and I.

I was always impressed by my grandfather's height and good looks—he was the son of a Chinese merchant—but both my grandparents spoiled me, and there was nothing they wouldn't do for me. I remember coming home from school one day for lunch and finding elephant fish soup waiting for me. Elephant fish are one of the biggest fish found in Tonlé Sap, Cambodia's "Great Lake", but I had heard a local tale about a dead woman who was reborn as an elephant fish, and I was horrified at the thought of drinking the soup. I cried and knocked the bowl over, and was punished for the first time.

My father heard about my tantrum and decided to take things in hand. I was sent back to live with my parents and soon discovered the limits of my freedom. I had to change schools and was separated from my classmates. I was also asked to do household chores and help my mother look after my little brother. Like all children, I was very sensitive to injustice and tried to stand up for myself, but my parents thought I was headstrong and insubordinate. Answering adults back is considered deplorable behaviour in Khmer culture, where children are expected to be submissive to their father up until they are married—a union almost always arranged by one's parents.

After I finished my third year in secondary school, my father decided to send me to Battambang Provincial

Centre to prepare for my Baccalauréat[1]. I was 16 years old at the time. In those days, girls my age usually stayed with their parents and didn't pursue any further education, but my father—who was a teacher himself—decided I should study for the Baccalauréat like my brothers. This was a very modern idea for the time, I wanted to study to get a better life than my mother, also to learn a new life. My parents rented an apartment next to my cousin's apartment, and he agreed to supervise me. Those three years away from my parents taught me how to live by myself and be independent.

After the Baccalauréat, I wanted to continue my studies in Phnom Penh[2] and train to be a doctor. My parents told me this career was only suitable for men, however, because it meant having to work at night, and this presented too many risks for a young girl. The science faculty didn't appeal much to them either, because boys and girls had to work closely together there. In the end, they settled on the law faculty. The sombre look of the building inspired confidence in them, and the students—already bonzes or civil servants—were much older and thus posed little threat to my innocence. This is part of our culture, even today, and I respected my parents, so I had no difficulty embarking upon the career they chose for me.

---

1   TN: Secondary school leaving certificate.

2   Phnom Penh became the capital of Cambodia in 1866 under the reign of King Norodom. The location is well-chosen for the political, administrative and economic centre of the country: at the heart of the most fertile plains, it enjoys the huge fluvial communication facilities of the Mekong River, accessible by sea in all seasons.

My mother's eldest brother, whom I simply called Uncle, put me up throughout my college years. He had been trained in a military academy in the United States during the 1960s. We lived in a villa in Abdulkarim Street in the Psar Kap-Kô market quarter, south of the Independence Monument. He was a colonel in the Supply Corps of the Royal Cambodian Army, but he was more at ease in an office than in military operations. As far as my grandparents were concerned, however, he was the image of success. He was accompanied by soldiers on all his trips and, to them, that was very impressive.

Uncle had two wives, and at that time he lived with his first wife, Aunt Ly, with whom he had no children. He had married his second wife, Aunt Dy, who lived in another part of the city, because Aunt Ly hadn't borne him any children. Bigamy was still legal at the time, and the 1967 Civil Code recognised both the first and second wives. For two years, Aunt Ly had been having serious health problems. She had cancer of the uterus, and a month before the fall of Phnom Penh in April 1975, she was operated on in a private clinic in the city. The doctors told us she wouldn't survive, and her health continued to deteriorate after the operation. She needed morphine every day to relieve her pain. Her nurse, who lived in the central market area, had to come every morning to administer the drug, and she sometimes came two or three times a day when my aunt's pain was most intense.

We knew my aunt was dying and had to come to terms with that fact, but it presented us with another problem: what would we do with her remains? While the rest of us were Buddhists, Aunt Ly was a nonbeliever and didn't want to be cremated. Strictly speaking, tombs are not allowed inside Buddhist monasteries, so we came up with an alternative solution. We decided to build a *chetdei*, or small tomb, for her in the Toeuk Thla pagoda beside Highway Five (which runs from Phnom Penh to Thailand), and hide it under a funerary *stupa*[3]. This became our main focus for several weeks and distracted our attention from almost everything else that was happening in the city at that time.

From 1973, Phnom Penh was no longer a safe or pleasant place to live. The city had become huge, and there were now well over a million inhabitants. The population continued to grow every day as more and more people came from the provinces to seek refuge in the capital, and the streets were crowded with the soldiers of General Lon Nol's[4] Republic. The hospitals were full of the wounded, both soldiers and villagers, and danger was all around us. The city had become claustrophobic, and I felt as though we were living in a hole like rats. I often heard B52 and other planes bombing in the distance, especially at night,

---

3   A *Stupa* is a funeral monument generally found within pagoda compounds.

4   General Lon Nol (1913–85) became defence minister and army chief of staff in 1955 in Norodom Sihanouk's government and served as premier under Sihanouk between 1966 and 1967. In 1970, he was responsible for the US-backed coup that deposed Sihanouk. He abandoned Sihanouk's policy of neutrality in the Vietnam War and backed the US and South Vietnam. He attempted unsuccessfully to suppress the Communist guerrillas, and plunged the country into civil war. In 1975 he fled to the US when the Khmer Rouge takeover was imminent.

and every so often I'd hear gunfire, sometimes far away, sometimes quite close to the city. The country was at war and there was no escaping it.

We celebrated the Khmer New Year on April 13, 14, and 15 of 1975 and had no idea it was to mark the beginning of Year Zero, the beginning of Pol Pot's social revolution in which every vestige of previous regimes was eradicated. I can clearly remember the morning of 17 April in Phnom Penh. Some of the public administration offices, as well as several universities and schools, had been closed the day before. I hadn't heard any gunfire or bombing that night, but I heard lots of cars and people on the move. My aunt was very unwell and hadn't slept, so I was woken early to fetch her nurse with my uncle's driver. At around 6 a.m. we were on Sisowath Quay, which runs along the west bank of the Tonlé Sap River, and is lined with vendors' stalls, hotels, restaurants, bars, cafés, and shops. Royal Marine patrol boats were docked in front of the Royal Palace just a block west of the quay, and a white flag was raised above the palace.

The streets were filled with young soldiers of between 16 and 18 years of age, all dressed in black. They were strolling calmly around the Independence Monument[5], the 20-metre tall, lotus-shaped *stupa* made of red stone

---

5   The Independence Monument was erected by King Sihanouk's father, King Norodom Suramarit, in 1958 to commemorate Cambodia's independence from France, which was granted in 1953. Today the monument serves as a memorial to Cambodia's war dead and is frequented by tourists and the city's teenagers.

that stands on the intersection of Norodom Boulevard and Sihanouk Boulevard in the centre of Phnom Penh in small groups of no more than ten. Others headed for the centre of town in trucks, and people of all ages came out to watch and to welcome these new arrivals. Here were two different worlds, side by side: on the one hand, exhausted refugees looking for a safe place in the city, and on the other, young republican students applauding the passing trucks and crying out things like, "Long live peace—the war is over!"

Further on the city seemed asleep. We arrived at the nurse's house without encountering any trouble and took the same route we had come by to get home. After the nurse administered Aunt Ly's injection the driver dropped her home again, and my aunt was able to rest a little thanks to the magical effects of the drug. In the distance I could hear cries of joy and people applauding, as well as the racket of trucks full of Khmer Rouge soldiers. Our neighbourhood was still quiet but, a couple of hours later, anxiety began to grow, and our neighbours started locking their doors. We still had no new information about the Khmer Rouge's victory.

Later that morning, at around 9 a.m., someone knocked loudly on the steel fence surrounding our house. The driver went out to see what the matter was and told us there were soldiers outside who wanted to talk to us. My uncle was afraid because of his status as an officer and didn't want to meet them, so I went out. There were four of them. They announced that we had to leave the house immediately because the Americans were going to bomb the city in a short while. I told them we had a dying woman in the house and were in an awkward position. I don't remember exactly how I addressed them; I may have said "Monsieur" or "Little Brother" or *mitt*, meaning brother. I felt a rising panic but tried to observe them discreetly. They were young; I guessed between 15 and 18 years old. They seemed tired, and were wearing *krama* around their necks. Their skin was as dark as their uniform, and I realised immediately that they were country people. They remained silent and serious, their faces impassive, their eyes empty. They showed no happiness in their victory, and in a few short words they told us to leave the house. The order didn't seem to brook questions or argument—no dialogue was possible. They left without those words of politeness or goodbye that Khmer people learn from a very young age, and this gave me the shivers. Uncle and I talked about the meaning and consequences of their message. We already knew that leaving would not be easy, but we were naïve and imagined the evacuation was perhaps a precautionary measure against the people in our area, which was posh and sheltered important national institutions and government personnel.

It was about 10 a.m. when a second group of four or five young soldiers arrived. They knocked loudly as before, and the driver again opened the gate. I summoned up the courage to go and see them while Uncle stayed out of sight. Again they said the Americans were going to bomb the city and that we had to leave the neighbourhood immediately. They added that we would be able to return in three or four days' time so there was no need to take our belongings with us. This second group behaved as impassively as the first, and the soldiers were completely devoid of emotion. Soon after they left we heard rifle fire in nearby streets, and this really frightened us. We decided to go to my other uncle, Uncle Phorng, who lived near Pet Lock Sorng, a bonze hospital opposite the Royal University of Phnom Penh, along the road to the international airport. There were quite a few of us: Uncle, Aunt Ly, myself, the driver and his wife, as well as their eleven-month-old son, plus our housekeeper and her 16-year-old niece. We brought enough luggage for three days. I grabbed a few items of clothing for Uncle, my aunt's medication, and a few things for myself—sarongs, shirts, and trousers—while the housekeeper prepared the rest of Aunt Ly's things. We didn't take any food, cooking utensils, or plates. Uncle was very frightened; he didn't look like a soldier. He took only money with him and, ironically, what worried him most was the fact that he had a pistol and an AK47 rifle in the house. Even though these could have protected us, he knew that weapons might give away his status as an officer in the army. He ended up leaving them in the wardrobe in my bedroom. I had rarely seen him leave the house without his weapons, and it was obvious that he felt lost without them

It was 11 a.m., 17 April 1975. Without realising it, we were leaving our house in Psar Kap-kô forever as we drove away in the Peugeot 405. We soon learned that the order had been given to chase everyone in the city out within 48 hours. Sick people, children, the wounded, the elderly, pregnant women—everyone was sent away without exception. Phnom Penh emptied like a body losing blood.

CHAPTER 3

DEPORTATION, 17 APRIL 1975

*Cut straight into the root! What's the point in questioning the
leaves and branches?*

Khmer proverb

Once we left the house, the Khmer Rouge
soldiers allowed us no freedom, directing us in
an authoritarian manner. We took the Preah
Norodom Boulevard and crossed the Chroy-A-oak
Bridge towards Koki. Our progress was slow because the
roads were crowded with people coming and going in all
directions. The scene was one of panic and confusion: old
people trailed along at the side of the road, too feeble to
keep up with the crowds; children cried out and clung
tightly to their mothers; pregnant women walked slowly
and with difficulty, their husbands and family members
urging them on; the sick and exhausted sat on the edge
of the footpaths watching as the city was drained of life;
some families pushed carts filled with furniture and

mattresses, while others were crammed into cars filled to bursting point.

The city was emptying in a cloud of dust; it was like an anthill suddenly being abandoned. Some people rested in public buildings along the roads, such as the university and the Beoung Trorbek high school. We had to hang around for a while because Uncle wanted to wait for Aunt Dy. She lived east of the Olympic Stadium and was to meet us on the same road with my younger brother Kolbotr and our cousin Thlay from Siem Reap, who were both living with her at the time, as well as her servant Huort, and her and Uncle's four children. There were now fifteen of us fleeing in all, ten adults and five children.

We spent that first night on the road, sleeping on a mat spread over a footpath. In the evening, only the children broke their fast, and our sleep was fitful and restless. When we rose the following morning, the scene was just as confused as before, and no-one knew where we were supposed to go. Announcements began to be made throughout the city on loudspeakers. We were told: "Inhabitants of Phnom Penh, our capital city has just been liberated by the brave and victorious revolutionary armed forces of Democratic Kampuchea." The Revolutionary High Command gave orders to the whole population to leave the city immediately: "Leave the city. Imperialist Americans are going to bomb it. You must evacuate the city before nightfall; we are under threat of bombing by American aggressors. Everyone must take the Chroy-A-oak Bridge before nightfall. Follow the instructions of the just and visionary victorious army. Move forward on Highways Four, Five and Six."

An order to hand in weapons was also broadcast every five minutes. We couldn't understand what was happening: after winning the war, why did we have to leave a liberated city, a city which should have been celebrating? We followed the crowds as they evacuated the city and our progress was much the same as before. Announcements were also broadcast over the radio, and we were warned that Khmer currency, the riel, would no longer be valid in a few days time. Everyone rushed to buy as much as they could in the markets along the roads, which quickly led to shortages. Each day we met more and more people leaving by car, scooter, bike, chariot, rickshaw, or simply on foot. Sick people lay on their wheeled hospital beds, which were now being pulled and dragged along the roads— some still had drips attached. We exchanged news with the people we met, and heard that Khmer Rouge soldiers had started killing higher public officials, particularly superior officers. Phnom Penh radio kept broadcasting news about the glorious victory of 17 April, the retreat of the Americans, and the fall of Phnom Penh. "The resistance has won the war. It is under the authority of the Angkar Pakdekvat [the Revolutionary Organisation] whose decisions are intelligent, crystal clear and fair. The people are victorious."

In the beginning, we had trouble understanding this new line of discourse, but we quickly grasped that the Angkar was the supreme authority which led the destiny of Cambodia, and had the power of life or death over each inhabitant. For the first time we heard the terms "*pror-chea-chun-chas*" and "*neak-moul-than*", meaning "Old people", a term the Khmer Rouge used to describe the population living in zones liberated before 1975. We were also introduced to the term "*pror-chea-chun-thmey*", meaning "New people", which described the population living in zones liberated after 17 April 1975 and, in particular, the population of Phnom Penh. The Khmer Rouge also used the expression "*kmaing*", which means "traitor", but this was also unfamiliar to our ears. We discussed what it was supposed to mean, but it would be several months before we fully understood the meaning of that word.

We continued to make slow progress as we attempted to leave the city, and the roads were barely visible under the swarm of human activity. The Khmer Rouge soldiers regularly went through our luggage, and they stopped and searched us several times before we reached Koki, a tourist resort located 12 km east of Phnom Penh. They especially wanted weapons, radios, watches, fabric, clothes, and medication, and they were requisitioning means of transport such as cars, scooters, and bicycles. When they wanted our goods they simply said "the Angkar demands it", adding the word "*dak-ruom*", meaning "pooling" or "sharing". Sometimes they demanded something precise: "Do you have an Orient brand watch?" or "Do you have a radio?" Anyone resisting confiscation was punished and beaten right in front of us, or executed in a nearby ditch by a shot from a pistol. I could hear the shots being fired, and when I looked into the ditches, I saw the bodies of the dead lying where they fell. I couldn't believe what was happening. We were powerless to resist the Khmer Rouge, and I felt sick to my stomach with terror each time they approached us.

People from Phnom Penh started hiding their valuables like jewellery or dollars in their underwear, or in a belt rolled around their body, because the Khmer Rouge hadn't started doing body searches yet. Under a hot April sun, many people were wearing several layers of clothing to hide their things. Most of the Khmer Rouge soldiers were uneducated peasants and couldn't read, so once they took our goods they weren't even sure how to use them. We wondered whether they were confiscating our things because they coveted them, or whether they wished to abolish all signs of our bourgeois lifestyle.

Although it was only a short distance from Phnom Penh, it took us four days to reach Koki. City people regularly visited Koki at the weekends for rest and relaxation, but thousands of people had already arrived before us, and the buildings and houses were already occupied. We knew this time our visit would be far from relaxing, but we hoped we would only have to stay a couple of days. We eventually managed to find some space in a traditional wooden house, which we shared with three other families from Phnom Penh. We tried to find out about the political situation in the country and what we could expect for the future. When would we be able to return to Phnom Penh? And where did we go from here? How would we be able to live? What would become of us tomorrow? Some people said we would not be allowed to return to Phnom Penh, and that we would have to go off to the country to work with the Old people. Most of us didn't believe this could be true, however, and we told ourselves it was impossible. Since the Khmer Rouge had won the war, why would we have to leave our homes? Now that the war was over, we would obviously be at peace again. I was still too young to understand this new invisible power, and even though I listened to these discussions, I didn't dare take part in them.

Thousands of people took shelter everywhere and anywhere they could: inside abandoned houses, beneath those houses, in make-shift tents, and even under big trees. The weather was hot and humid and we felt very uncomfortable. The land around Koki was rich and fertile, and each year it produced a multitude of fresh vegetables and wonderful fruits such as mangoes, jujubes, jackfruit, star apples, sapotes, sugar apples, and other wild fruits. Within a few days of our arrival, however, there wasn't a single fruit left on any of the trees; the refugees had picked them all, ripe or unripe. Water was also in short supply and the situation became increasingly acute. It was the hot season, which meant the water in the nearby river was low, and it quickly became polluted as more and more people tried to wash themselves and their clothes in it. There were also very few proper toilet facilities and, like cattle, both adults and children excreted in the open air. All over the ground, excrement and urine produced a fetid odour, and the stench became unbearable.

After several days of waiting, we had eaten everything to be found in Koki; there were no supplies left. The riel was worth nothing, and it was very difficult trying to feed a family of fifteen. Aunt Dy was the only person in our family who possessed a great fortune, and she had managed to bring all her jewellery with her from Phnom Penh. We had hoped her wealth would help to ensure our survival, but she categorically refused to trade any of her possessions for food. I began to trade my own clothes—especially the most sought-after things such as sarongs and shirts—for rice, sugar, meat, fish, or vegetables. Soon there would be nothing left to trade.

Aunt Ly's state of health became more and more alarming. She could no longer feed herself and there were no doctors in Koki to help us. I had managed to sneak some morphine past the soldiers but I had never given an injection before. I tried to copy what I'd seen the nurse do, but we soon ran out of the medicine. The pain Aunt Ly was suffering, the fact that she could no longer move, and the worry she saw overtake the rest of us, became too much for her. She lay impassively day after day and had trouble speaking. We waited for her to die.

My young brother Kolbotr and our cousin Thlay wanted to leave Koki and join their respective families back in Siem Reap. My father had died of illness five years before and our mother was now alone in Siem Reap with nine children, six of her own and three nephews; we knew she must be really worried. Without a man to help support the family, their survival in a situation like this was uncertain, so Kolbotr and Thlay headed off.

My brother was short-sighted and wore spectacles. He loved long hair, something our father had never appreciated, and wasn't afraid to be different. Some time later he was spotted in a village on the road to Siem Reap, his head partly shaved, probably already condemned by the Khmer Rouge. According to the Revolutionary Angkar, people who wore spectacles like him were intellectuals and had to be eliminated. We never saw my brother again. I couldn't bear to think about what might have happened to him.

A few days after Kolbotr and Thlay left, our driver and his family left us too; we had no further news of them.

A month of waiting went by, without any hope of going back to Phnom Penh. Little by little people left for different destinations and the rainy season began. This was the monsoon period. Fewer and fewer people remained in Koki and food supplies were more and more difficult to find. Often, Khmer Rouge soldiers hunted us away. All hope of returning to Phnom Penh slowly but surely evaporated.

During this waiting period, those who had the means tried to find a way of going abroad, preferably to Vietnam because it was close, and because there were fewer landmines on the eastern border than in the Thai border zones. We also heard that people were escaping by boat on the Mekong River. Uncle and Aunt Ly thought we should try to escape to Vietnam first, and then go from there to another country. They thought we would be able to rely on Aunt Ly who spoke Vietnamese fluently and had some family in Saigon. Aunt Dy, however, wanted to go to Thailand where she had been born and raised, but the idea of escaping to Thailand with a family of ten people seemed impossible to us. It was much too far to travel on foot, and too unsafe given the Angkar's vigilance. We knew we would never make it so we abandoned the idea. Uncle, as head of the family, now had a difficult decision to make: try to escape to Vietnam or go home to Siem Reap. We had heard that Khmer Rouge soldiers guarding the Vietnamese border zone were killing people they found attempting to flee to Vietnam via the Mekong River, and that the Vietnamese arrested those who managed to make it across, so finally, Uncle decided it would be safest to join our family in Siem Reap.

This meant abandoning the car he loved so much. Before we left it we removed everything we thought we would need from it for daily use: the seats, the mats for sitting on, and so on. The journey to Siem Reap turned out to be extremely difficult. Aunt Ly could not walk at all and the children were too young to walk such a distance —over 200 km. We needed a cart to transport my aunt and the little ones, and I agreed to trade a gold bracelet I had, as well as some sarongs, to buy a wagon and some other provisions for the long trip. To reach Siem Reap, we would also have to pay for a boat to take us to Rokakong[1],

---

1   The village of Rokakong, which has been under Khmer Rouge administration from 1973, has been described as a sacrificial village, see *Procheasas* (research group), *Cambodge, population et societe aujourd'hui*, L'Harmattan 2005, p. 250.

a big commune[2] in the province of Kandal, located on the banks of the Mekong River. Uncle and I made a stretcher from two bamboo trunks and a rice sack so we could move Aunt Ly to the boat.

The day of departure for Rokakong finally arrived. We woke at dawn, and my little cousins cried because they were hungry and didn't want to walk. First we loaded up the little ones and then Aunt Ly into the boat. Since this was only the beginning of the rainy season, the river bank was still firm and the water was low. Uncle, the housekeeper, and I carried Aunt Ly on the hastily-made stretcher. In order to reach the Mekong River itself, we first took the Bassac and sailed towards Phnom Penh, the river stretching its four streams like arms before the Royal Palace.

The city was deserted. There wasn't a sign of life except for a few members of the Angkar working on the banks of the river. It looked like a place stricken forever. We sailed away from Phnom Penh on the Mekong, our stomachs in knots and tears in our eyes.

The Mekong River was splendid and calm, and as we sailed I wondered what was happening to the Khmer country, a country that had gained its independence from France without conflict or confrontation. The Khmer

---

2   Translator's Note: to avoid confusion with municipality, township, etc., the (French) word "commune" has been retained throughout. It is close to the Khmer word—*khum*—and is used in English on the Cambodian government site. A commune is the third administrative division (after province and district). A district consists of 11 communes, each of which represents from three to thirty villages. A village ("phum") is the basic administrative subdivision.

people are said to be peaceful but courageous, fearless, and proud. They are attached to their customs and traditions, but love to laugh, and have a wonderful sense of humour. In our current circumstances, I wondered whether it was possible to preserve our peaceful nature, and memories of childhood ran through my mind.

In the 1960s, our country was at peace, and when we went to bed at night we left our doors unlocked. If a traveller arrived, he was well received and fed heartily. The land was generous, and the rivers were clean and full of fish. We waited for rain, and if it didn't fall, we held a festival and prayed to the rain-god, an ancient animist tradition that Buddhism hadn't managed to wipe out. When the rains eventually came, the snakehead fish left the ponds and wriggled across the streets, where the children danced and played in the puddles. I wondered what remained of all that now. What would the future hold for me? As we sailed in the small, flat-bottomed pirogue towards unknown territory, the future seemed very bleak indeed.

I remembered being taught the anthem of the *Sangkum Reastr Niyum* at school. This was the "People's Socialist Community", a movement created in 1955 by Prince Norodom Sihanouk. For him, it was a question of committing to the construct of a neutral and socialist state, while defending it from communism. At the same time, however, Prince Sihanouk was getting closer to China. At the end of 1960, in order to protect himself from his Vietnamese and Thai neighbours, the prince signed a Treaty of Friendship with China. He took a further step in the direction of China on 3 May 1965, when he broke with Washington. At the beginning of 1963, Saloth Sâr, the future Pol Pot and leader of the Angkar, Ieng Sary (Brother No. 3) and So Phim (Brother No. 4)—the incarnation of a radical and procommunist opposition—left the capital to join the resistance. This was the time when the Cambodians, originally Chinese, claimed to be more and more Maoist, and favoured rupture with the Sangkum.

I was far too young at the time to realise that war was on its way, and the period between 1955 and 1970 was above all a period of happiness for my family. But the clouds were gathering above our country. Prince Sihanouk had a premonition of this and gave a cinematographic preview of it in his film, *Shadows over Angkor*, in which a young army officer tries to foil a coup that was being hatched with foreign powers.

Compared to its neighbours who were tearing each other apart, Cambodia looked like the Switzerland of South-East Asia. That was how General Charles de Gaulle described it in 1966. I was in my first year of secondary school at the time, and together with all the pupils from lower secondary school, I was brought to Siem Reap to welcome the General at the airport. We formed a guard of honour for our guest, crying, "Long live General de Gaulle! Long live Franco-Cambodian friendship!" General de Gaulle was in a convertible with Prince Sihanouk, and he was so tall that he seemed supernatural to us. It was said that a special bed had to be made for his stay. That night I returned to Siem Reap with my parents, and my brothers and sisters, to attend a procession of elephants accompanied by torchlight on the path to the temple at Angkor Wat. That was the first time I had seen such a large procession of elephants, as in Khmer tales from long ago. On the river, *pirogue* races were organised in keeping with the tradition of the Great Water Festival. Later, on the radio, we heard General de Gaulle's famous speech in which he pronounced these prophetic words: "While the kingdom advances on the right path, that of neutrality, why does war at its borders provoke an outburst of killings and ruin which threaten its very future? Yet there is no chance that the peoples of Asia will submit to the law of a foreigner from the other side of the Pacific, no matter how powerful his weapons." To us secondary school boys and girls, the General was like a demigod, in the same way that the temples built by our ancestors were magical, because we believed in all those supernatural powers our elders spoke of.

The coup was about to take place. Early in 1969, Washington set off a campaign of aerial bombing in the provinces close to South Vietnam. On 18 March, Marshal Lon Nol and Prince Sirik Matak took over power, backed by the American army, and relieved Prince Sihanouk of his duties. In spite of itself, our country became the field of confrontation between the USA and the forces of North Vietnam.

I remember the air attacks and the exchanges of gunfire in the villages near Kralanh where I was born. Sometimes my father would go and spend the night with friends who lived outside the village, fearing that he might be requisitioned if he stayed at home, because Lon Nol's army had to make up for people deserting its ranks. The teaching body to which he belonged, because it was close to the socialist movement, was often threatened by the authorities of the Republic. So my father hid.

Later that morning, we were still on the river, moving further and further from Phnom Penh. The riverbanks slid by in muffled silence and four hours later, we arrived at the Rokakong pagoda, one of the great pagodas of the region. To get Aunt Ly up onto the bank, we again had to lift her in the make-shift stretcher. In the pagoda, dozens of families were waiting to leave for destinations that were becoming less and less safe. Only a few bonzes remained and we asked permission of their leader to lodge under the *sala,* the communal meeting room of the monastery. Our accommodation was more comfortable than our shelter in Koki. We had three bamboo beds: one for Aunt Ly, the housekeeper, and her niece; the second for my uncle, Aunt Dy, and their youngest daughter; and the third for me and the other three children. Trading was still allowed here and we enquired about exchanging our clothes for rice and food. Things like long-sleeved shirts, sarongs and black or dark fabrics were considered of value, while Orient-brand watches were the most sought-after objects by the Angkar and the Old people. They were worth more than the gold and precious jewels women didn't dare wear any more. A gold chain of five *chi* (about 18 g) was now worth scarcely more than 6 kg of hulled rice, and a diamond ring was worth about the same. As more time passed, however, the value of jewellery lowered even further because the Old people had less and less merchandise to exchange, and they knew that the *dak-ruom* project (the pooling of goods) was about to be put into practice.

Rumours circulated in Rokakong. We were told we could pay fishermen who knew the rivers well to take us by motorboat to the Vietnamese border. Once more we discussed our options, and this time Aunt Dy didn't hesitate; she was prepared to go to Vietnam and find a way from there to another country. But how could we travel with Aunt Ly? Uncle made some enquiries and found a small fishing boat that could take us. We paid for the boatman and the fuel with our clothes and jewellery. But on the eve of our departure, we heard that the Khmer Rouge had arrested and killed any New people who attempted to escape. As for the Vietnamese, they had reinforced their border checks, leaving no chance for survivors of the Khmer Rouge regime. We had no choice but to cancel our plans and we lost the money we had paid to the smuggler.

At this stage, Aunt Dy got actively involved in bartering. She did well too, meeting several people she had known in Phnom Penh. She immediately started her own business, not only to make enough to cover our immediate family needs, but also to make a little profit with each barter, as some other speculators from Phnom Penh were doing. But Aunt Dy wasn't careful. One day she was trying to trade a piece of gold jewellery with a man, and she took the jewellery out of her bra where she normally kept it hidden to show it off to him. The man looked closely at the jewellery, but said he needed more time to think about whether he wanted to trade for it or not, and went away. That night it was particularly hot and humid, and Aunt Dy didn't put on her precious bra as she usually did. Instead, she hid the bra and her jewellery among the rest of her clothes which she kept in bed with her as she slept under a mosquito net. When she woke up the next morning, the bag containing the jewellery had disappeared. We searched everywhere for the bag, and found it several hours later behind a *stupa* inside the pagoda. All the contents but the precious bra remained. This was a terrible blow for our family. Until then, we had depended on the valuables Aunt Dy had kept. I had just one small gold chain and a few pieces of clothing left, while Aunt Ly and Uncle had only a diamond ring and a watch between them. We had traded everything else.

Aunt Dy was very quiet about the theft and didn't even want to talk about it with Uncle. As his second wife, she had less of a claim to his money than Aunt Ly, even though she was the mother of his children. As the Khmer proverb says, "When you have children, you think further ahead," and she had taken precautions in case anything serious happened to her husband. She had thought that, at the very least, she could count on her jewellery if she ever had to start afresh and pick up the pieces again. In the end, however, Uncle and Aunt Dy decided to report the theft to the authorities of the Angkar in the village. Two or three members of the local authorities came to register the report and proceed to an inquiry. Afterwards, other New people told us we shouldn't have declared a loss of valuables to the Angkar, but it was too late. Their complaint had given the local authorities information on our bourgeois background, and we became terribly worried. Uncle and Aunt Dy were sorry they had said anything to the authorities and were now afraid for their lives and for ours.

At the same time, Aunt Ly's state of health declined even further. She was now very weak and couldn't eat. She often lost consciousness, and on a July morning in 1975, she passed away. We buried her in the presence of the few remaining bonzes in the pagoda in Rokakong. Because we were so terribly afraid, the grief caused by the loss of a loved one didn't seem quite so hard to bear. We felt that on leaving us, Aunt Ly had escaped further suffering and would not have to put up with the Khmer Rouge regime like us. In our culture, death is seen as a liberation, and we often say the deceased person has "gone to heaven." We had to accept Aunt Ly's *karma* and our own, and in a way we were relieved that the responsibility which had weighed so heavily on us was lifted. Soon after Aunt Ly died, our housekeeper and her niece asked for leave to join their families. They had stayed with Aunt Ly to the end.

The rest of us now had to prepare to continue on our trip to Siem Reap, but we had no food left. Uncle went looking for a bicycle to help us pull the cart. The Old people knew the Angkar would soon remove private ownership of all property, buildings and otherwise but we, the people from Phnom Penh, couldn't imagine such a thing happening. It seemed completely unrealistic. We got a bicycle in exchange for several items: Aunt Ly's diamond ring, a few sarongs and several shirts. Now we had a rare means of transport, and the bicycle would help us to trade. When Uncle came back with the bicycle I could see the happiness on his face. This city bourgeois had abandoned all his possessions, and now an old bicycle gave him enormous pleasure.

Barter in Rokakong became more and more difficult because the Old people had nothing left to trade. We knew we had to go further afield to trade with other villages if we were to survive. Aunt Dy wanted to go with Uncle but she didn't know how to ride a bike so he decided to take me with him instead. We only had a few items left to trade and we hoped to use some of them to get rice, which had become the last thing in the country of any value. With rice we could buy meat, fish, vegetables and everything else. For the first time since we left Phnom Penh, my uncle and I were happy to go looking for rice. The villages along the Mekong River are very pretty and varied, and cycling was one of the few pleasures we had left. At first Uncle pedalled and I sat behind him but before we had even covered 1 km, he was tired and it was my turn to cycle. I didn't last long either and we changed places several times before we arrived in the villages of the Old people. We met a few New people on the same mission as ourselves and in the afternoon we started trading by going from one house to another to find buyers. In the afternoon we managed to get about 60 kilos of rough rice.

We arrived back in Rokakong exhausted and our family were relieved to see us. We were as happy as if we had won the lottery and would be able to survive for at least another couple of weeks with the rice we'd gotten. Even so, we couldn't help wondering what would happen to us when there was nothing left to trade. What did we do then? But for now we concentrated on hulling the rice. This was a tough job and only Huort, Aunt Dy's servant, knew how to do it.

Huort was originally from the province of Siem Reap and my mother had recruited her a few years before to work for Aunt Dy. Like us, she wanted to go back to her family in Siem Reap. I had heard that several families who left Phnom Penh with their servants encountered problems because the Angkar considered this type of relationship to be slavery, and it had to be punished.

To hull the rice, Aunt Dy borrowed a *tbal-ken*, a little rice mill, from a villager behind the pagoda, and the three of us worked at turning this home-made appliance. Once we had separated the grains from the paddy ball, we whitened the rice in a mortar or *kdoeurng* which is specially designed for this purpose. Finally we separated the bran from the hulled rice using a round basket with holes in the bottom. By making circular movements with our hands the whitened rice separated from the bran which was too big to pass through the holes in the basket. We repeated the entire process several times and after a half day we had managed to prepare 10 kilos of white rice, a very small yield to feed all of us. We worked at this almost every day for several days.

For the next trade, we tried a village even further away. But rice was now more and more expensive and increasingly rare. The monsoon rains were well under way and the rust-coloured mud on the lanes was very slippery. We put a heavy sack of rice on the bike, and moved forward slowly and painfully. My uncle slipped and fell several times, taking me with him. We were not used to walking in mud and found it difficult to keep upright and push the bicycle as well. We were obliged to spend the night away from Rokakong and a family in the village we eventually made it to kindly put us up. Our clothes were damp and our hosts lent us dry clothes and gave us a meal. The next day we thanked them heartily and went back to the pagoda in Rokakong. Aunt Dy had been worried about us and was relieved we had made it back safely, though unsuccessfully. We had a little palm sugar left and Aunt Dy found a coconut. It was an ugly coconut but we made do with it and made a very simple dessert, *borbor skor*, a soup of sticky rice, coconut milk and palm sugar. The dessert was delicious and brought back family memories. We may as well as have been eating *bay-dam-noeub-san-kya*, a luxurious dessert loved by most Khmer, which is prepared with glutinous rice and flan, and melts in your mouth. This reminded me of the Khmer saying: "When you are hungry, everything tastes good. When you're in love, everything is pretty."

Rumours continued to spread that the Angkar had abolished house-workers and servants because it considered this kind of work to be human exploitation, and everyone had to manage on their own under the new regime. Since we had come to Rokakong, I noticed Huort's behaviour had become odd. She didn't listen to us any more, and didn't want to do anything we asked her to. She was often absent for several hours at a time and wouldn't tell us where she'd been. We had presented her to the Angkar authorities as a relative, but she began to differentiate herself from us in many ways. I had a feeling she was going to leave and was afraid she might have told the Angkar authorities that she worked for us, and given them details about our background. My aunt and uncle felt responsible for her, however, and it was their wish to keep her with us and bring her home safely to her parents.

One day a representative of the revolutionary authorities came to the pagoda and told us that Huort had to join the Angkar because she was not a member of our family. Huort seemed delighted with this, and from the time she left us, she was completely transformed. She now only ever wore black, with a red and white *krama* knotted around her throat, like the cadres of Democratic Kampuchea. Every so often we'd see her driving a horse and cart along the road in front of the pagoda but she never looked our way. From then on, she would have to make decisions about her own future and fate.

Her departure put our family at great risk, however, and terrorised Uncle and Aunt Dy. Between the report they'd made to the authorities about the stolen jewellery, and Huort's revelation that she was not in fact a member of our family but our servant, they were really frightened. The combination of these facts formed sufficient evidence to confirm that we were New people, and by now we were sure that the Angkar authorities were eliminating intellectuals and the middle-class. This included students, officers, high and medium state employees and other white-collar professionals. The New population had to hide all clues that might give away their identity, and the Khmer Rouge soldiers spotted the well-to-do and middle-class by their lighter skin or their different attitudes. There was no room for us in the "glorious future" reserved for the Old people.

Little by little, the deportees who had stopped at the pagoda in Rokakong moved on. There was no hope of going back to Phnom Penh, or of being integrated where we were because Rokakong was no longer receiving New people, so we decided we had better leave, and soon. We knew it was just a matter of time before the authorities of the Angkar came looking for us and we were not sorry to be leaving Rokakong. This was the place where we had lost everything, where Aunt Ly passed away, where the housekeeper, her niece and Huort had left us, and where Aunt Dy's jewellery was stolen.

We kept our plans for departure secret from the other villagers and made our preparations discreetly. We were like prisoners planning an escape and didn't even tell the children. We needed at least 50 kilos of rice to get to Siem Reap so my uncle and I left to trade in the surrounding villages. We took everything we had left that might appeal to buyers but this time trading was much more difficult. The conditions were changing every day and the barter market was drying up. We managed to collect 45 kilos of hulled rice but we had to trade everything we had left for it. The next morning we made ready to depart and woke the children at 4 a.m. We left without a sound.

On the road, we were the only ones going anywhere. The rest of the New people were already installed in the various collectives set up by the Angkar. From time to time we saw people working in the fields under a blistering sun and knew it might only be a matter of time before we were forced to join them. In spite of everything, however, we were optimistic about our departure and hoped the road to Siem Reap would lead us to a better future.

PART II

THE BLACK PERIOD

CHAPTER 4

THE EXODUS OVER, THE TRAGEDY BEGINS

Without family or marriage, no justice and no society.
                                                    Proudhon

After four or five days' journey we arrived in Phum Thmey in the province of Kampong Cham. We were exhausted and hoped to find a place to rest but as soon as we stepped foot in the village, Khmer Rouge soldiers stopped us and said we didn't have written authorisation to travel as far as Siem Reap. They then declared that New people like us had all been integrated into the Old people and whether we lived here or in Siem Reap would make no difference since the Angkar would look after us. They placed us with Mr Chourp and Madame Pheap, whom the villagers at the time called Ta (Grandfather) Chourp and Yeay (Grandmother) Pheap. The village had already received 100 New families and this was a heavy burden, but Ta Chourp and Yeay Pheap, who had a large family of six, welcomed us without any animosity, unlike some of the other families who were forced to take in New people. They lived in a wooden house on stilts and gave the back section of their home to Uncle, Aunt Dy and the children, while I had to share a mat with their single daughter, Phann.

Phann took after her mother and was eager, bright and talkative. The new regime had transformed her status from daughter of peasants to "daughter of the Angkar" and, like all the Old daughters, she had become mistress of herself and of the land for the first time in her life. As a daughter of the Angkar she was separated from those who hadn't yet acquired this status and had the right to special privileges concerning work, food, health care, and visits to her family. She worked in the *korngchalat* of Old girls whose treatment was much less harsh than that meted out to the New girls. Phann didn't show any superiority towards me, however, and treated me like a sister.

My family and I were immediately placed under the supervision of the authorities of Phum Thmey and the day after we arrived in the village we had to report to the village chief and the *sahakor* director to register our family. The registration process took the whole morning and we were asked to write a biography for each member of our family. The authorities were particularly concerned with where we had come from and what Uncle and Aunt Dy had worked at before 17 April 1975. They told the authorities they were shopkeepers and that I was a pupil in my final year, but the authorities misunderstood them and thought I had only completed first year in primary school. This seemed to satisfy them.

The next day we were transferred to different work groups and were separated according to our marital status and according to our sex. Uncle and Aunt Dy joined separate male and female groups of married persons while I joined the group of single girls, which would later be transformed into a *korngchalat*. Uncle was given the responsibility of pumping water into the nearby paddy fields with a home-made apparatus invented by the cadres, while Aunt Dy had to grow tobacco, and I had to transplant *décrue* rice plants[1]. Sometimes Uncle had to plough the paddy fields, and every so often Aunt Dy had to mind children, harvest sweet potatoes or peanuts, pick vegetables or hull rice for the sahakor. Neither of them had the slightest experience of this kind of work and it did not come easily to them.

In the beginning, each adult received a food ration of about 250g of rice per day while the children, who didn't have to work, were given only half that amount. We were still allowed to cook for ourselves, however, and after our first day of work we came together to eat. Uncle was exhausted and told us he didn't like the work, and Aunt Dy admitted the same thing, but we had no choice concerning what we did anymore.

---

1 TN: these are planted in moist soil after flood water recedes. The French word "*décrue*" has no suitable English equivalent, although the terms "dry season rice" and "rainfed rice" are sometimes used.

The alluvial areas of the Mekong make the soil in the province of Kampong Cham very fertile and all along the Mekong River people grow rice, tobacco and vegetables such as aubergines, peppers, tomatoes, and Chinese melons when the water in the floodplains recedes. All of these have a short cycle and require a lot of water. My work varied according to the needs of the *sahakor*: transplanting rice, harvesting tobacco leaves, harvesting rice and corn, or building dykes.

The first task I was appointed, however, was transplanting rice, which was hard work for anyone not used to it. Transplanting could be done alone or in multiples of two, depending on how many workers were available. For the Angkar, this was a collective task and we had to line up side by side in groups. For every round of planting we each took about five rice plants, holding them in our left hands and transplanting them with our right. Up until the end of 1970 many varieties of rice were grown but the Khmer Rouge only authorised the cultivation of rice with the highest yield; varieties such as floating rice, and all other varieties had now disappeared. The seeds were sown very densely in nurseries, where they were sprouted and made ready for transplanting. Once three or four rows were planted, we had to back out quickly before the mud sucked us in. With each round of planting we sank further and further and very quickly the mud would reach to our thighs. It was difficult to stay upright in these conditions and we had to be careful not to lose our balance. I saw many girls from Phnom Penh retching and crying when they were forced into the paddy fields, but no one dared to help anyone else anymore. We had to manage alone.

Transplanting was exhausting work but if we didn't plant the rice quickly enough, the other girls would back out behind us and leave us alone in the middle of the paddy field. The daughters of the Old people laughed at our progress. They were much faster than we were and would back out sooner, planting more rows behind us as they went. When we tried to back out after them we knocked over the plants behind us and had to plant them all over again. This was the hardest thing of all to take, and we were ashamed of ourselves, but the daughters of the Old people showed us no compassion. They felt only hatred and contempt for us.

When I woke the morning after my first workday I could neither stand nor walk. My legs, arms and hands were swollen like tires. In spite of this, however, I managed to adapt to this new way of life more quickly than some of the other girls, and soon I could plant as quickly as the Old girls. Several New girls from my *korngchalat*, however, were only familiar with products from city markets, and had no idea how rice or vegetables were grown. When we pulled weeds in the paddy fields, they were incapable of distinguishing the rice plants and pulled everything in their path.

Even though the work was hard in the beginning and many of the girls struggled to acclimatise to this new way of life, the cadres still afforded us a little time to ourselves after lunch. I used my free time to make clothes such as shirts, trousers or even underwear ordered by the Old people. I also made pretty hats from young palmyrah palm leaves. Both the Old and New people loved these and I exchanged them for rice, fruit and other foods. For about three years, well before the fall of Phnom Penh, the villagers hadn't been able to go to town to buy clothes, medication, small cosmetics like lipsticks, perfume, shampoo, soap, toothpaste and so on, because the Khmer Rouge had already started supervising them and restricting their movements. They missed all these things terribly. Modern-style clothes brought by the New people were worthless, however, because they didn't correspond to the dress habits permitted by the Khmer rouge, except for a few long-sleeved shirts and sarongs. The most modern clothing allowed now for women was a mandarin-collared shirt with long sleeves and a *sampot*, which is a traditional wrap-around cloth worn on the lower body, or elasticated trousers. For the men the most modern outfit was a western shirt and elasticated trousers. All the clothes were dark or black. Female cadres wore a black *sampot* to the ankles and a long-sleeved shirt so that neither their arms nor their necks were visible during meetings or official ceremonies. They only ever wore a short-sleeved shirt in the evenings, while the *korngchalat* girls wore only trousers and long-sleeved shirts. I was young at the time and at an age when normally you want to look good, but these desires were completely extinguished.

It was dangerous to be different under the new regime and as a New girl I tried to blend in as best I could with the Old girls, which meant drastically altering my appearance. Old girls from my *korngchalat* were nice to me and generally treated me well because I worked hard, but they laughed at some of the other girls for being too pale. I was also much paler than the Old people and realised quickly that I would have to get a tan in order to fit in. So I exposed my arms and face to the sun as often as I could to darken it like the chiselled skin of Old peasants from Kampong Cham. I dyed all my brightly-coloured clothes with the fruit of the *makleur* which Khmer peasants use to blacken fabric. I wore a *krama* both at work and after, and wore Ho Chi Minh sandals cut out of old tires, or failing that, sandals made out of light wood. I cut my hair short and carefully banished all city elegance from my behaviour. The Old girls told me my first name was too long to pronounce and looked like the name of a bourgeois foreigner. They suggested the name "Tha" and from then on everyone called me "Borng Tha", which meant "Sister Tha". Family names no longer had any value, since we were all now part of the Angkar's family. Suddenly, I felt everything had been taken away from me: my family, my studies, my personality, my habits—even my name had disappeared. Nothing remained of me and this gave me the shivers. For a time I was completely traumatised and disconsolate, but I had only one objective: I wanted to survive so I could see my mother and my family again, and I was determined to fight to the bitter end.

The Phum Thmey authorities made us write our biographies at least three times during the month after our arrival in the village, and each time, Uncle and Aunt Dy declared they were shopkeepers. My ability to keep up with the work in the fields assured them about my background, but they had concerns about Uncle and Aunt Dy. From the beginning of their integration, they couldn't bear the collective work and complained every day that they had stomach cramps from hunger. They were very depressed and regularly asked permission to stay away from work on the pretext of looking after the children. Other times they simply tried to escape from their places of work. I often heard the Old people making remarks about them. They said they were sérei, which means their behaviour was "free". This was a serious accusation and I was very worried about it. Sometimes at night I heard Uncle and Aunt Dy talking about great meals they had eaten in good restaurants in Phnom Penh, served with good wines and whiskey, and I was terrified they would be overheard. The Khmer Rouge cadres told us constantly that we had to forget everything that existed before 17 April 1975, and they repeated the slogan "the Angkar has as many eyes as a pineapple" to remind us of the many spies they had placed amongst us.

At night, the Angkar militia hid surreptitiously under our houses or outside our walls, and listened to our conversations. These were mostly young combatants of between 15 and 17 years of age, whom the *San-tek-*

sok[2] had put in charge of spying on the population, transporting ammunition and eliminating civil servants, soldiers of the old regime, "New" people or even cadres who were under suspicion. It was the Angkar militia who took members of our *korngchalat* to be executed if they suspected them of being New people or intellectuals. While we were at work, they came and went between us and sometimes pretended to work with us so they could listen to our conversations and watch our behaviour. I heard many rumours that the militia were *dach-khat* people, which meant they executed without question on the orders of the Angkar.

But we were all hungry, and it was difficult not to think of the past. None of us had enough rations to assuage our hunger and we never stopped thinking of food. I especially thought of Chinese noodles and nice desserts, but Ta Chourp and Yeay Pheap's daughter Phann was good to me and often gave me a bowl of rice with a little piece of dried fish, or a piece of sweet potato, to ease my stomach. Some people in the village too gave me fruit or other food from time to time.

Just three weeks into our stay in Phum Thmey, the rice ration of 250g per person was reduced. We now received only 400g of rice per day for the whole family. The children fought with each other at every mealtime when the rice was shared out, and my youngest cousin was already suffering from malnutrition. She was often ill, constantly hungry, and ate everything she could find:

---

2   These were security and police forces installed in each commune.

raw rice, grains of salt, raw fish and any other food stuffs she happened across. I now posed a serious problem for Aunt Dy, and one day Yeay Pheap told me a secret: when I was at work, Aunt Dy prepared an extra meal for the rest of the family, even though we didn't have enough rice for two meals a day. This performance didn't escape the pineapple eyes of the Angkar, however. They noticed that I was the only one in our family who worked in the first unit, the unit with the hardest labour, and they came to the conclusion that I was being exploited by my uncle's family.

Hunger destroyed everything: honesty, bravery, family feeling. No one could rely on their family any longer; we could trust no one. Family bonds were gradually weakened before they were done away with completely. Children no longer needed their parents because they were children of the Angkar, and they no longer lived with their parents; they lived in a centre for children and were brought up by the Angkar. All over the country, the Angkar used children to spy on their parents and families.

The Old people in the village told me I shouldn't live with my uncle's family any more, that the Angkar could ensure my living. I didn't make any decision, but I knew Uncle thought of Aunt Dy and his immediate family first. Only after that did he think of me. By then this behaviour was normal for me, but I could still remember the conversation between my mother and Uncle when she sent me to live with him in Phnom Penh. They agreed that he would take care of me like his own daughter and my mother would do the same thing with his children who lived nearby with my grandmother in Siem Reap. But this commitment no longer meant anything. I knew my uncle and his family didn't need me any more because I could no longer help them. And I no longer needed them. Tension had grown between Aunt Dy and me, and from time to time Uncle intervened between us in favour of his wife. I had already lived alone during my final three years of secondary school in Battambang, and I knew that I would soon have to leave Uncle and Aunt Dy and join the *korngchalat*. I could no longer consider my family as a refuge so I got used to the idea of living separately.

A couple of weeks later, news circulated in the village that New people were being expulsed. One afternoon while we were at work in a paddy field not far from the village, the head of our *korngchalat* called the names of four or five girls who were to leave immediately with their families. The girls left without a word and we never saw them again. When I got home in the late afternoon Uncle, Aunt Dy and the children were gone. I was told they had left for Korng Ta Noeung, a village in the district of Korng Meas, but from then on no one ever heard of them again. I was now alone, without family or friends. I had nothing left. According to Buddhist rule, my future was behind me and I had to give in to my karma. But I knew I had to hang on. I thought of my family in Siem Reap and hoped I would see them again.

One day soon after Uncle and Aunt Dy had left, a couple of peasants came to visit Ta Chourp and Yeay Pheap. They had come to propose marriage between their son and me. We had both been students in Phnom Penh and ran the same risks. His parents thought we'd be safer if we were married and that we would avoid the hardest work camps. This proposition surprised me; I had never dreamed of getting married in such a situation. Once the visitors left, Ta Chourp and Yeay Pheap argued that this proposition was good for me, and that I would be able to live in the village and have a family with a man who held the same status as me, but I couldn't decide what to do. A few days later, the young man visited me, accompanied by his sister and in the presence of my foster family, as custom required. He was tall and good-looking, with pale skin, but he was shy and only said a few polite things. I needed time to think.

I still felt too young to make a decision like this. I lived alone in a family that wasn't mine, in the middle of a communist society which had deprived me of all freedom. Even though Ta Chourp and Yeay Pheap were very kind to me, I didn't consider them to be my adoptive parents. I felt like someone who had been set adrift. How could I make such a decision without the advice of my family? I'd been brought up in a culture that insisted on parental consent to marry. But at that moment, those principles hardly served any purpose, and I had to protect myself in order to survive. After giving the matter some thought, I agreed.

His parents set the administrative procedures with the Angkar, personified by the village chief, in motion. The young man and I didn't live in the same village, so the authorisation took a long time. Two months later, the answer came back and it was a refusal. We were not yet sufficiently reconstructed and did not merit marriage. The wheel of the Angkar continued to turn and shape our destiny, like the cycle of samsara in the *Buddhist* religion.

CHAPTER 5

POOLING EVERYTHING

When the waters rise, the fish eat the ants. And when the waters recede, the ants eat the fish.

Cambodian proverb

"You mustn't hide anything you possess from the Angkar. Absolutely everything belongs to the Angkar". That was the Angkar's motto.

As we tried to settle into this new regime the Angkar began to adopt more and more extreme policies. We received new orders from the cadres that we had to pool all our goods. The Angkar was attempting the complete dispossession of a people and no citizen was allowed to keep anything whatsoever for themselves. All goods had to be handed over to the Khmer Rouge authorities: houses, land, cattle, rice, jewellery, means of transport, tobacco, fruit trees, fowl, even the vegetables grown in the garden, clothes, fabrics, stoves, old pots, dishes . . . everything. The deadline for the pooling of all movable goods had been established. Everyone had to commit to it with a responsible attitude and offer their goods to the Angkar for common collective use from now on. With one simple order, all private property was abolished and the Khmer Rouge carried out the Angkar's orders with exacting precision.

In the cooperative created by the Angkar, two or three members of the Phum Thmey authorities took care of registering the objects which the Old and New people came forward with. We New people didn't have many possessions left because the Khmer Rouge soldiers had searched our luggage, and helped themselves to whatever they liked, in each village we'd travelled to since we left Phnom Penh. In the beginning the Khmer Rouge cadres sometimes bartered to take things they liked, such as clothes, jewellery, or medication, and they gave food in exchange. After a while, however, they ordered us to simply abandon our belongings, using the term "*chum-rouh*" which means "to dispossess of everything". Members of the Angkar came to take whatever little we had left while we worked in the fields, and the cadres frightened us by saying the authorities had metal detectors to find our jewellery so it was useless to try to hide anything. According to the Angkar, jewellery was "a capitalist item which poisons society completely", but they used it to buy weapons in China so they could go to war against the Americans. Some people observed the rule and pooled their jewellery, but others kept it hidden, figuring that though they couldn't wear it, it might help them to survive. Among us, only our *korngchalat* leader still dared wear small earrings, pretending she had to keep the pierced holes open. The Khmer had learned from their ancestors where to hide their jewellery and they had many hiding places: buried in the ground, sunk in the well, walled up, hidden in a bamboo or in the trees, especially those where palm-sugar juice was collected. Those who hid their belongings, or didn't want to pool them, were enemies of the Angkar and risked their lives if they were ever found out. As the Angkar motto put it: "He who protests is an enemy, he who opposes becomes a dead body."

Once they had taken all our possessions, the authorities issued an order to some of the villagers to dismantle their houses, and to use the reclaimed wood to build a collective kitchen and storehouse. The villagers had built their homes themselves and it pained them to see them simply torn down, but they had little choice in the matter and reluctantly complied. Out of sentimental attachment they inscribed their names on the individual pieces of wood that came from each house, a small reminder of their old way of life. The authorities grouped the now homeless families together and issued an order to build small houses around the cooperative. The idea was to put the cooperative at the centre of daily life, further destroying the concept of individual families.

The Khmer people had always remained close to the land of their ancestors, and in the old days families depended on their properties to survive. A piece of land with a few palmyrah palms and the presence of a family *stupa* nearby were sufficient conditions for their attachment to the land. The palmyrah palms provided not only food, but the raw materials necessary for building and thatching, as well as making baskets, fans, hats, umbrellas, and so forth, and very few Khmer people left their villages to settle elsewhere. The sharing of goods under the terms of the Khmer Rouge destroyed all this and removed the foundations of familial and societal organisation. Private property was reduced to "a single bundle" containing only a few pieces of clothing, a plate and a spoon. In some villages the Angkar had *kum-rou* houses built. These were small wooden buildings on stilts, four metres square and without a kitchen, covered with tiles or thatch. They gave them to the Old people or to couples who had been newly united by the Angkar, and this type of building still exists in some parts of Cambodia, such as the commune of Sranal in the Kralanh district of Siem Reap.

This was just the beginning of the Angkar's system of sorting and purging. Men, women, and children were regrouped according to their sex, age, matrimonial status and whether they were New or Old. We were classified and organised like objects on the shelves of a haberdashery. So I, a single, New woman, was integrated into a *korngchalat* for this category. There were about 120 of us in all—110 of us New and the remaining 10 Old. The New girls in our *korngchalat* formed a unit of first strength, and were under the supervision of the Old girls. The other daughters of the Old people, including Phann, were integrated into a korngchalat for single, Old women and received better treatment than us. The hierarchical chiefs in every *korngchalat*, however, were systematically chosen from amongst the lowest classes—uneducated peasants without land or property—and these new leaders suddenly found themselves in positions of authority, without any experience. They quickly discovered their power and used it without restraint, like children running free with weapons. The aims of the Angkar were clear: to dispossess the upper classes of their power and authority and give it, without any preparation or education, to the least well off and least educated. The Angkar created a situation whereby the Khmer Rouge cadres could exact their vengeance on the upper classes whom they despised with unfettered violence.

The work regime got progressively harder and nobody took an afternoon nap after lunch any more, a custom normally respected by Khmer people and accredited as the "secret of long life". Not even the Old people dared to take a nap and work started again as soon as we finished eating lunch. But the married people were able to go back to their families at the end of the day. I was still living with Ta Chourp and Yeay Pheap. I spent my days working in the fields and slept in their house at night. A short while after being integrated into the *korngchalat*, I was transferred to work in a sewing workshop of the cooperative. This new work was less painstaking than the work in the fields and I much preferred it. But it wasn't to last. A month later the cadres sent me back to the work camp and I learned afterwards that the Old people couldn't bear to see me working in the shade while their children worked in the hot sun. The village chief shared their sentiment and so I went back to working in the fields with the other New girls.

Meanwhile, the sorting of New people continued and a collective model of life was put in place. The cadres announced that soon the collective kitchen would be installed and our life would be easier; the women would no longer have to prepare meals or look after their children, so they would be available to work outside the home. The collective kitchen would distribute two meals per day, lunch and dinner, to those of us who worked, and we were no longer authorised to prepare food for ourselves. Nothing of our former world now remained, except we ourselves, living people who were the object of constant purging and elimination. With a few simple orders the Angkar had re-invented everything and from now on everything belonged to the Angkar. Any kind of exchange was strictly forbidden. Gathering fruit, even if it was at the house where you lived, or fishing in the river, were considered acts of theft and were punishable by death. Over and over again, the Khmer Rouge cadres reminded us that absolutely everything belonged to the Angkar.

A few days later, the collective kitchen went into action for the first time in our village. Around 11 or 11.30 a.m., the gong heralded the collective meal and we ran towards the kitchen. We lined up to get rice, one ladle each, and the cooks served us soup at a long wooden table. Everyone from the village had come to eat, and music composed by Angkar musicians was broadcast over loudspeakers. The cadres told us the collective meal was a festive occasion and we would celebrate like this every day. The cooks didn't go to much trouble, however; they threw a few bits of fish or meat into boiling water with a few vegetables and that was it. Traditional Khmer cooking, made with a judicious combination of vegetables, flowers, fruits and spices, was but a memory. The famous *prahok*, a fermented fish paste in brine, garlic and Kampot pepper, was gone. Often the cook's limited the meal to transparent soup which was far quicker to cook, but from time to time the odd fried vegetable appeared. Though the cooking was mediocre, for the moment at least, it was sufficient to feed us.

Some of the Old people were able to conceal certain food supplies such as rice, sugar, beans, corn, coconut and dried fish in their houses. Although absolutely forbidden by the Angkar, they quietly gathered the fruit and vegetables which grew around their houses. When the collective dish didn't appeal to them, they asked for permission to eat their ration at home, and ate the other food stuffs they had collected. Ta Chourp had formerly had a little land but it was too small to cover the needs of his family and they had always been poor. He was quiet and silent, like an old peasant, and his attitude corresponded well to what the Khmer Rouge expected of the Old people. He often said we had to obey the Angkar and its cadres and never dared complain, always minding his own business. His wife was franker and more talkative. Sometimes she complained about this new life and about the fact that everything was in short supply. Occasionally, hunger pushed her to break the Angkar's rules and she gathered fruit in her garden or killed a chicken so her family had some evening soup. Each time she broke a rule, Ta Chourp told her off quietly because he was afraid. He believed all the bad luck they had was due to the *karma* that follows you like your shadow, and resigned himself to bad *karma*.

The camp cadres announced that in compliance with a new order, each *korngchalat* was to be shared out according to the needs and targets of production set by the Angkar. My work camp was to join Zone 41 and erect new dykes, dams and bridges as well as transplant and harvest rice. The canals and dams were 10 km long and we worked over 12 hours a day, sleeping in shacks at the edge of the work sites. We ate in communal canteens, wore the same black clothes and Ho Chi Minh sandals, and both men and women had their hair cut short. This standardisation was impressive: you saw only people in black everywhere, in dark *krama*[1], with the same type of sandals, all over the country. It was a strict way of life and the birth of a new people. We were repeatedly told that there were neither poor nor rich, neither exploiters nor exploited, and that we were all equal under the new regime. But we realised that we were an inferior group. On the site, discipline was formidable. Whether it rained or whether we were sick or tired, we had to work like machines.

---

1   traditional Cambodian multipurpose scarf.

We were watched constantly throughout the day and were overwhelmed by work. Each evening the cadres made us go to meetings of criticism and self-criticism, and invited us to adopt a "fair attitude". They told us, "The woman or man of 17 April must detach him or herself from parents, family, friends, house, goods and even his/her personal effects." We had to give up everything so we could be better integrated into the Old people. Each night we hunkered down and, facing the other members of the *korngchalat*, we had to confess our weaknesses, our behavioural failings, our laziness, and our regrets. Each one had to take his turn and admit to the theft of an ear of corn or a banana, to taking an unauthorised break on the worksite, or to nostalgia for the past. Each one of us was pressurised to denounce traitors, and telling on friends was a way of improving one's image. Whether the criticism was founded or not, the criticised person had to thank the Angkar for it and make a promise to improve.

We were repeatedly quoted the declarations of Pol Pot, Brother One and leader of the Angkar, though at the time we didn't know who was leading us. We were told, "For over 2,000 years our people lived in the greatest destitution, despair and discouragement... If our people were able to build Angkor Wat[2], then they can do anything. Thanks to the Angkar, the living conditions of the country are going to take a great leap forward . . ." We were told

---

2   Angkor Wat is part of a temple complex at Angkor in Cambodia. It was built for King Suryavarman II in the early 12th century and has remained a significant religious centre since its foundation. The temple is the epitome of the high classical style of Khmer architecture and appears on Cambodia's national flag.

that our revolution had overtaken that of the Vietnamese and the proclamation of the superiority of the people of Kampuchea over the Vietnamese was recited like a song. Our successes were continually repeated: "The evacuation of Phnom Penh, the abolition of corruption and money, the institution of a collectivist regime—forever." The Angkar taught us to work with fervour for the economic revival of the country. We were called upon to be "determined to reinforce our revolutionary watchfulness and to think of our elders who faced the war and brought us victory". Did our leaders believe this? Some probably did, but the words didn't carry any weight with us. Nothing in the Angkar's words resembled our reality.

One particular day I was working with the *korngchalat* of New girls; we were building a little dam in Phum Thmey and had been divided into small groups. Four girls were digging the soil and eight of us were carrying the clay to build the dam. I carried the earth in a basket of woven rattan, leaning it against my hip as I walked back and forth. I was coming and going all day, and the rhythm was monotonous. Suddenly as I walked past the line of girls digging the soil, I felt a sharp pain in my right hand. One of the girls had accidentally hit me a blow of her pickaxe. There was a large open wound on the back of my hand, and even though the pain was excruciating, I tried not to cry out. I was scared of the cadres and covered the wound with my scarf. Some of the girls came to see what was wrong and they took me on foot to see the only nurse left in the commune. His name was Mr Proeurng and he was known throughout the commune for his efficiency and good humour. When he saw me, he told me I had extraordinary luck because in a few days he was leaving to join the villagers in the men's section of the married people's camp and would no longer be authorised to practice medicine. He disinfected my hand with alcohol and then closed the wound with a needle and thread. There was no anaesthetic and it hurt more than anything I had ever experienced but I put up with it, with tears in my eyes. After this accident I was forced to rest. The pain continued all night and I didn't sleep a wink. The next day, my hand was swollen like a kapok doll. Mr Proeurng told me to clean the wound with boiling water and salt twice a day, and three days later the wound started to heal. Little by little it closed up but I could feel a sharp stiffening in my hand when I tried to stretch my fingers. In a week, the wound had closed up and I took the stitches out myself. I am right-handed and couldn't do much with my left hand. I had difficulty dressing, washing clothes and even eating during this period, but the children of Ta Chourp and Yeay Pheap helped me out, even helping me to dress.

A month went by like this, and I still couldn't use my right hand. The wound was still tender and painful but the leaders of the *korngchalat* and the cooperative were contemptuous and blamed me for the accident. When I went to get my food ration at the collective canteen, they said I didn't deserve it any longer, and I hated the way they looked at me. I was sent to the leader of the cooperative to ask for work which corresponded to my newly handicapped situation and I was given permission to work in the shade at the cooperative headquarters with the married women. The work was more varied. Sometimes I was asked to sort tobacco leaves or to dry and hull rice that was to be stocked in the cooperative granaries. I got more and more used to using my left hand but when I opened my wounded hand it was still stiff. I was not allowed stay and work in the cooperative under the reproachful eyes of the Old people for very long, however. According to the Angkar, we had to "identify malingerers and eject them from the community." As the Khmer Rouge often reminded us, "*Tuk min chamnenh, yok chenh min khat*", "Keeping you is no gain, destroying you is no loss."

CHAPTER 6

THE ANGKAR PLOUGHS THE LAND AND REAPS ITS LIVING SOULS

Whoever is without shame, will be shameful at his death.

Khmer proverb

For many peasant farmers, the Prince was still the earthly representative of the gods. All power emanated from him, even justice. But nobody knew if Prince Sihanouk was still in his palace or if he still reigned, and nobody mentioned him. It was customary in our country not to ask questions of the hierarchy, and this rule of silence suited the Khmer Rouge perfectly.

After the takeover of 17 April 1975, the army melted into the population, and into the administration of Democratic Kampuchea. There was no longer any ranking or stripes in the army, and the Khmer Rouge soldiers were among us, watching our every move. In the villages, they stepped in at the call of the *korngchalat* or cooperative chiefs to accomplish missions like "the elimination of a

New family"—a term used by the Khmer Rouge—or to "*fight* the transplantation of a rice field or the harvest". The Angkar no longer hid its determination, and violence crept into our everyday language. Those who disobeyed the Angkar were the *kmaing*, the traitors, and this word was endlessly repeated. Our cadres now talked openly of *kam-chat*, the elimination or execution of the Angkar's enemies and traitors, and we heard verbal threats at every evening's meeting.

We never saw any tribunal, but we knew there were prisons. They were euphemistically called "offices", but in reality they were places of detention, investigation, torture, judgement, execution and also the headquarters of the *San-tek-sok*[1], the regime's instrument for getting rid of opponents. The members of the security force had one main mission: to find the "enemy within". The definition of an enemy was very broad and meant anyone who might displease or harm the Angkar. Enemies and traitors were defined as those who were not active; those who didn't obey the leaders; those who made mistakes at work; those who looked for extra food; those who were ill or absent from work for several days; those who didn't want to work; or those who arrived late to work. According to the revolutionary doctrine of Democratic Kampuchea, the enemy counter-revolution had to be fought continuously. Purging of enemies was called *boh-sam-at*, which meant "to sweep away" or "to clean up". The objective was to guarantee party security and maintain the purity and

1   security force. The *San-tek-sok* played the role of political police and spy-watchers.

perfection of the revolution. This was what we heard in all the speeches. We were taught to work conscientiously and devote our efforts to the service of our people, our country and the revolution. We were not to ask anything of the Angkar because the Organisation had thought of everything and knew everything about us.

Another month went by and my *korngchalat* was moved to the village of Antong Sar more than 10 km from where we had been staying. I stayed behind because of my injury, but when my wounded hand pained me less, I asked for permission to rejoin my *korngchalat*. I was afraid to linger for too long in case I aroused suspicion. It was nearing the end of 1975 and I had begun to notice a class system similar to the caste divisions in Brahmanism emerge around me. There were now three separate groups with very distinct privileges and rights: the cadres or members of the Angkar formed an elite ruling class, the Old people became a sort of middle class, and New people like me formed the lowest class, and were burdened with the most difficult and menial tasks.

At my level, power was mostly given to young people of modest origins, who came from other regions, or to Old people from neighbouring villages. These Old people were given leadership roles and positions of influence. They had lots of privileges that were denied to us. When the daughters of the Old people were ill, for example, they were authorised to rest for longer than the daughters of the New people. When they went to see the nurse from the Angkar, she would discreetly slip them some imported medication to treat their illness, but when we went to see her we got only pink or white tablets manufactured by the young workers in the laboratories of Democratic Kampuchea. We referred to these as "rabbit-droppings" because they cured nothing.

In the same fashion, the right to visit one's relatives was given to the Old people with greater generosity and indulgence, whereas we were almost always denied visits. We all ate, both New and Old, in the same collective canteen, but the daughters of the Old people received extra food rations from their parents when they went home at night. The daughters of 17 April 1975 were deprived of everything and treated like slaves. We were criticised violently by the camp leaders and by the Angkar cadres because we were brought up according to bourgeois and capitalist principles, and didn't know how to work in rice fields. We had not been part of the revolution of the Angkar, and were progressively rejected, accused of being lazy and soft, of living from the exploitation of the blood and sweat of the poor, and of behaving like leeches. Every evening after the meal, everyone had to attend a meeting of criticism and self-criticism, which often finished late. No one could escape except the meetings for exceptional permission which we didn't dare request. The criticisms were always centred on the same subject, the class of the New people, their re-education and the liberation of the peasants. I sensed hatred growing around me, and I heard the same criticism in the men's camp and in the married people's camp.

Not far from us lived a woman named Kim Touch. She had lived in Phnom Penh with her husband, who was a soldier in Lon Nol's army, before they were deported in 1975. They decided to go to a cousin who was a peasant farmer in a village near Phum Thmey. At the time she was pregnant with the couple's second child, but her husband was murdered by the Khmer Rouge a few weeks after their arrival in the village. Shortly after giving birth, she was ordered to carry and hull rice. Then she had to join the group of "newly married" who were in charge of ploughing, a practice that has changed little over the centuries. All over Cambodia you can find agricultural tools which have changed little since Angkorean times. In particular these are: the plough, with a metal sock, this is drawn by a pair of oxen or buffalo; the cart, light, solid and entirely made of wood; the sickle with a short blade, very practical for harvesting rice. Nothing was spared these men and, above all, women of the New people, a people condemned to disappear once they had been exploited to exhaustion. In the beginning, as a city-dweller, she couldn't manage the plough. But the threat of death hung over her constantly, and she told herself she had to survive.

She knew well that she was being tested, because in Cambodia it is only the men who work the soil, while the women do the transplanting. However, under Pol Pot's new regime men and women were equal at work, whatever their physical strength. That is why women were obliged to climb to the top of Palmyrah palms to recover the sap, a task normally only done by trained men who made a career of it.

Kim Touch was assigned two oxen, but all cattle looked alike to her, and she had no idea how she would distinguish her cattle from the others. During her midday meal she watched them constantly; if she lost one, or if one went and grazed on rice shoots, she knew she would be accused of treason. So a friend in her group explained to her that each animal wore a different dress, and she had to examine the dress well and memorise the characteristics of each animal. Little by little, Kim Touch adapted to the work and became an ordinary ploughman, thinking if she worked hard she would be spared. She worked the land in both her own village and in the neighbouring villages.

While working, she sometimes dug up a few sweet potatoes or vegetables which helped her to survive. As in our case, she didn't get enough to eat in the collective canteen. She thought that she worked harder as a married person than in a *korngchalat*, but she considered herself free to feed herself. Every day she was frightened that she would meet the same fate as her husband, but with the help of her cousin she managed to keep going. In contrast to many of us she didn't believe in *karma*. As far as she was concerned, the whole Khmer people had suffered this tragedy at the same time, and the merits of our previous lives had nothing to do with it. She also noticed that those people who hurt her didn't all suffer the same fate—some were dead while others had managed to survive. To fight for her own survival, that was her only wish, and good or bad *karma* had nothing to do with it.

The Angkar revolution was not an industrial one; it was concentrated on agriculture which was, according to the cadres, the engine of progress. The cadres were uneducated, most of them couldn't read or write, and they had no capacity for taking initiative or for reflection. They repeated what they heard at meetings with their superiors, and the Angkar was able to count on them because they carried out orders without any pause for consideration. At checkpoints, some cadres or soldiers read papers of authorisation upside down, and most of the time they didn't understand them. Nevertheless, they pretended to read them because Khmer people don't like losing face, particularly Khmer Rouge cadres in front of New people. I heard several stories of New people who falsified papers themselves so they could move from one village to another to visit relatives, or move to an area where there was more food, or where the elimination of New people wasn't as strict.

In my *korngchalat*, the Khmer Rouge cadres now put me in charge of counting the length of the dykes and dams, and the surface of the paddy fields, and writing reports to be sent to the Angkar *loeu*, the superior Organisation. The cadres remarked that I had good handwriting and asked me why this was. I told them it was hereditary, and my father wrote as well as I did without ever having gone to school. One woman, Madam Chhom Phirun, told me that Kann, the chief of the security force, and his deputy, Horn, were responsible for the army and for the prison of O Trakuon where the most atrocious executions in the district of Korng Meas in Kampong Cham took place. I was terrified that the young combatants of the militia would notice me and I would be sent to the prison for questioning.

The work became more and more difficult in our *korngchalat* and the purging of New people became more clear-cut. Each night the cadres got together, and each morning we'd receive new orders to achieve Angkar objectives. The revolutionary movement was operated like a well-oiled machine, and anyone who interfered with its functioning risked getting crushed between the cogs. Death sentences were handed out to those who committed acts of serious misconduct, such as several absences from a meeting of criticism and self-criticism, answering back a chief who criticised you, not working for a few days, stealing an ear of corn or a banana, having sexual relations outside of marriage—anything that displeased the Angkar.

On one occasion I witnessed the punishment of a woman from our *korngchalat*. She hadn't been feeling well and asked for leave to rest. The woman was hungry, and when she was alone she took some food from her friend's bundle. The leader of our *korngchalat*, Eng Heang, accused her of treason during the evening meeting, and slapped her in front of us. She kicked and beat the woman on her back and head with the handle of a flail. Eng Heang then ordered me to bring a cord to tie the woman up, and she spent the night tied up at our feet in the dormitory, crying silently. I wondered why our leader, a woman barely older than the rest of us, who knew the other woman's family well, had beaten her so easily and gratuitously. Where had such violence come from? It took me a while to realise that Eng Heang was protecting herself by showing her superiors that she too knew how to repress the slightest misdemeanour with violence. By punishing our colleague in such an ostensible manner, she probably helped her to avoid the much more severe punishment the soldiers would have given her.

On another occasion, Nany, a New girl from 1975 like me, was almost sent to O Trakuon prison, but was saved by Eng Heang. Her family lived in the neighbouring village of Phum Thmey. One day as she was coming back from the river after washing herself, she discovered a tree of ripe sugar apples and wondered why they hadn't been picked. They made her mouth water, and she decided to pick two of the fruit, but someone saw her picking them and reported her crime. That evening she was taken, her feet and hands were tied, and she was abandoned like that in the disused mosque of Antong Sar. She was very scared and thought she was going to be executed. The next day a girl from the camp just happened to come by, and Nany asked the girl to tell Eng Heang about her situation. Thanks to Eng Heang she was freed, and came back quickly to the camp. She was sure that if Eng Heang hadn't come to get her, she would have been sent to the prison at O Trakuon. A few years ago I saw Nany again and she told me that this event had marked her for life.

She still lives in the area and every time she goes past the mosque, she covers her face so she doesn't have to look at it.

Usually in the past when there was a festival, a marriage or a cremation, we played music. The songs, often composed from Ramayana themes, fed our dreams or eased our pain. The Ramayana is an ancient Sanskrit epic and is one of two epic Hindu poems, the other being the Mahabharata. The Ramayana describes a love story between Rama, an ancient King, and Sita, who is captured by Ravan, the King of Ceylon. Rama lays siege to Ceylon and wins back Sita. It is attributed to the Hindu sage Valmiki and forms an important part of the Hindu canon. Instead of the same old tunes of the crooners who nourished our adolescence, however, we now heard only the national anthem, "Glorious 17 April[2]", which called us to defend our fatherland and the revolution in martial tones:

> Bright red blood covering the towns and plains
> Of Kampuchea, our homeland,
> Sublime blood of workers and peasants,
> Of revolutionary men and women combatants,
> This blood of implacable hate and resolute struggle,
> On 17 April under the flag of revolution,
> This blood freed us from slavery.

---

2   Unofficial translation by the author.

Long live the glorious 17 April,
Brilliant victory shining brighter than Angkor times,
We come together to build the new Kampuchea and the new
shining society,
Democratic, egalitarian and fair,
Following the resolute path of sovereignty and independence.

We commit ourselves firmly to the defence of our homeland,
Our sacred, revolutionary and glorious land.
Long live, long live the new democratic and prosperous
Kampuchea,
Wave high the red flag of revolution
And build a homeland of increasing greatness and glory.

The blood of our people would indeed cover the countryside, in destruction of our youth and strength, and in complete contrast to the ideals of justice and democracy. In the year 1976, the battle was launched to make the best harvest, and much blood was spilled.

The middle of the Cambodian central plain is occupied by the Great Lake from which the Tonlé Sap River flows from west to east across the country. The Mekong River, which we also call the Tonlé Thom, irrigates this basin and is favourable for rice-growing. The Khmer Rouge constantly referred to the building of great works which would allow settlement in the flood basins and ensure a great leap forward for production. The paddy fields were now replaced by huge square plots of one hectare, and the year was organised around several cycles: the twelve months cycle and the binary rhythm of the wet and dry seasons. For the six months from May to the end of October it rains almost every afternoon, but it rains very little during the other six months. November and December provide a Mediterranean-type climate which the Khmer call *khè ka-dek*, and this period is more suitable for growing dry crops.

At this period of 1976, our entire cooperative was ordered to grow tobacco. We had to prepare the land as carefully as in a garden, and the tobacco plants were planted out in lines like the rice shoots. When it came to weeding, we were made to walk barefoot on thousands of earthworms, some of which got under our skin and made us ill. I had never seen so many worms as in the Kampong Cham region. Green melons, peppers, watermelons, and pumpkins were grown between the rows of tobacco plants, and when the tobacco leaves were ripe, they were harvested. In the village, the married women waited for the carts that transported the leaves, and when they arrived they started tidying them into bundles. The leaves were then put out to dry in a dark depot so they changed colour. We started work before dawn; the bell rang around 3 a.m. each morning, and the cooperative gathered its strength to complete the harvest which lasted for only a few weeks.

Again we worked in groups. The first group took out the leaves, the second group removed the stems and grouped the leaves, and a third group went over and back carrying the leaves to the men. The men chopped the leaves on a block of wood with a very sharp knife, piling them up as they went. The rolled the leaves along little by little with their left hand and cut them with their right. A final group was charged with spreading the cut slices on woven bamboo mats and leaving them out to dry. This delicate work was new to me and, in spite of its monotony, I found it a sort of distraction.

This was *raung* year (the name of a year in luna calender), placed under the sign of the Naga and our battle to complete the harvest continued. We now turned our attention to the rice harvest. "The water is great," as our elders said, and the Angkar objective was to have two rice harvests per year, then three, with a yield of between three to three-and-a-half tonnes per hectare. This had never been done before and, in order to complete the mission, all the front line forces from the single people's *korngchalat*, and the second line forces from the married men and women—made up of families of both Old and New people—were united. Everyone had to go down in the paddy field with orders for combat. I found the transplanting season the hardest of the year. We worked in the rain, and the food supplies of the previous harvest were by then very scarce indeed. "If you don't finish the work in the day you'll have to work all night," our leaders told us. The harvest season was only bearable because it gave us some hope of receiving better rations later on. I can clearly remember experiencing very cold weather between December and January during the Khmer Rouge regime, but that is how we felt our privation—

malnutrition made us more sensitive to the cold and heat.

We awoke before dawn each morning and were given just 15 minutes to get ready; then we had to go to our place of work. Each of us was equipped with a sickle and a length of cord to tie the animals and assemble the rice plants in the dry rice fields, plus a little bundle containing a can of boiled water, a spoon, and a plate. We attacked the transplantation on an empty stomach and pulled the plants to be transplanted. We pulled the young plants carefully and had to wash the roots in water by moving them around against our feet. We struggled with leeches in the rice fields but were careful not to show any fear because the Khmer Rouge reminded us that leeches had no weapons, and those who complained risked their life. When a leech sucked at our ankles, we tried to imagine it was merely an ankle bracelet, like the piece of jewellery called a *korng-chhloeung*, meaning "a bracelet in the shape of a leech". Some girls were very frightened and tried to remove the leeches with their sickles, wounding themselves in the process. These girls were then heavily criticised during the self-criticism meetings later in the evening.

Once we had finished pulling the rice plants, we transported them to the paddy fields for transplanting. Each girl had to have three or four *phlaunn* (forty units) of rice plant bundles. To transport a bundle, we lined up the rice plant bunches along a cord which was about three metres long. We then tied up the first bunch and rolled it along the line until the whole thing formed one huge bundle. We had to hurry because if we were last, we had to lift the whole roll of rice plants onto our head by ourselves, and it normally took two people to do this. Sometimes we walked as much as 4 km to and from the paddy fields, carrying the rice bundles on our heads. Each roll was heavy, weighing between 20 and 35 kg. We walked along very small and narrow dykes, and when it rained these were slippery and we often tripped. We weren't permitted to take the rolls down to rest our heads on the way because the work couldn't be interrupted. The cord which tied the bundles together left deep marks on my head that hurt for hours. Many of us had swollen neck glands and, after a day spent bent over in the rain, our hands were pale like those of a drowned person. Each evening our limbs were numb after hours transplanting in water. We walked day and night in the rain and were treated like animals. Not even the animals risked being killed when they got tired, however, and we were told over and over again, "You are not a grain of salt which melts in the rain."

As we were working to complete the harvest, we were also assigned other jobs, and my *korngchalat* was ordered to pull the stumps of trees to widen the space for the paddy fields. This was very hard work. The leader gave each of us between five and ten stumps per day depending on the complexity of each stump. To do the job we were equipped with a pick and a machete because the terrain to be cleared was usually covered with thorny wood and bushes. We dug around the roots of each tree and cut each root one by one, then knocked the stump over with the help of a neighbouring girl. Sometimes we were faced with trees whose roots went far too deep, and we were incapable of finishing the job. In these cases the leaders would give us something else to do; the main thing was that we be kept busy. Removing tree stumps was simply to avoid idleness when our job in the rice fields was done and served no real purpose. We were often asked to transplant rice, and then a few days later we'd be ordered to pull the plants we had just transplanted and re-plant them somewhere else. We went from one work site to another, from one combat zone to the next, without seeing any coherent plan. The work was aimed at pleasing the upper cadres and devised so it never stopped; we were kept busy day and night.

It was now the season of high water (between June and October), and the water was rising very quickly. The second line force couldn't cope with collecting the corn, and many fields were already flooded. The water in some fields reached to the workers' hips and in some cases even as far as their necks. So the cooperative asked for us to help. Our leader sent us to harvest the corn with the married people. Snakes, scorpions, ants, and every sort of insect were looking for a dry place to escape the water, and they hid in the corn leaves above the water. When we went to cut the stalks we surprised them, and they bit us terribly. In spite of all this, however, this work was a godsend for us because it meant we could try and steal some corn to alleviate our hunger.

During the time I spent in the *korngchalat* I managed to get close to some of the other girls, and one of my closest friends was a girl named Vanny. In 1972 when American bombings and attacks against the Khmer Rouge were becoming more and more frequent, her family left the commune of Rokakoy and settled in the town of Kampong Cham. Eight months later, in April 1973, Kampong Cham fell to the Khmer Rouge. The evacuation of the urban population ordered by the Khmer Rouge had been carried out under the same pretext of imminent American bombings they later used to evacuate Phnom Penh. Vanny's family fled again and went to join their extended family in Phum Thmey. From then on Vanny and her family were referred to as "New people of 1973".

One morning Vanny had to go to work while I was ordered to stay in the hut and do some sewing. I filled her can of boiled water for the day, and when she returned that night she had managed to fill it with grains of sweetcorn. Nobody had seen her take the grains and we were overjoyed at the feast before us. We grilled and caramelised the maize, and ate it in the night like thieves. It made a nice, crackling noise and sounded like the termites that ate our cabins every night. Whenever we were able to steal some corn we made little cakes with grated maize instead of glutinous rice, and wrapped them in banana tree leaves. These little moments of happiness lifted our spirits and helped us to hang on. Vanny and I got on well, and we tried to help each other as much as we could, but these moments were rare and food shortages were now a part of our daily lives.

"If you want to stay alive, work," said the Angkar, and we did work—morning, noon, and night. The main meal of the day was at 11 or 11.30 a.m. if there were no urgent jobs that needed doing first. At a signal from our leader we stopped working and each of us, armed with a plate and spoon, headed for the collective canteen. If we were working in the village we sometimes shared the canteen with the married people's *korngchalat*. Each day we queued up to receive a ladle of rice soup, either a clear soup or a thicker soup. Sometimes the soup was mixed with a couple of pieces of fish, pork, beef, or some fruit and vegetables such as Chinese water spinach, Chinese cabbage, young melons, banana tree shoots, bamboo shoots, young bananas, aubergines, or whatever else the cooperative had managed to collect. At other times we were given a ladle of red maize which, in the days before the Angkar, was normally reserved for pigs. Those who worked in the collective kitchen were charged with collecting food stuffs from the villagers, and they went from house to house collecting anything and everything they could. Many of the villagers submitted their produce to the cooperative of their own accord, preferring to hand over their goods voluntarily rather than being obliged to hand them up.

We ate our meals in small groups of about five people, sitting cross-legged in a circle on the ground. A tin bowl of soup was placed in the middle of the circle, and each of us plunged our spoons into this same bowl, without knowing our neighbours. Our clothes were often wet or damp from working in the paddy fields, and the soup tasted of rust from the metal bowls. The cooks always served themselves first and we knew they ate their fill. We thanked them, nevertheless, especially when they made an effort to cook a little more, or when they slipped a piece of meat or a spoonful of salt into our bowl. We often ate only water spinach soup, and the roots floated on top of the clear liquid. At other times our tongues and teeth were stained with black wax from plants that were too old or too dry. While we worked in the fields we tried to catch wild crabs and frogs, or collect edible wild leaves. We prepared these in secret at night and used them to complete the next day's meals. During the few weeks of the harvest we were allowed thick rice soup or *bai* which was more substantial, but the rest of the year we usually ate only corn soup mixed with a small portion of rice. Ripe red maize became our basic food; it helped appease our hunger but it was terribly hard and indigestible. Occasionally, we were given pieces of rotten fish which gave off a fetid smell, and I had to ask for extra salt to disguise the taste so I could finish my meal. We constantly glanced at our neighbour's bowl to compare if we had gotten as much as everyone else. Our hunger was huge, infinite, permanent. Only people who have suffered starvation can understand how all-consuming hunger becomes. We would have done anything to appease that pain which tormented us and get a spoon of sugar or a couple of bananas.

In the days before the Angkar's regime, people living along the Mekong had grown white maize for human consumption. It was soft and could be mixed with rice, but it was no longer grown because it produced a small yield. The cadres of Democratic Kampuchea also refused to harvest young and tender yellow maize because it couldn't be kept for too long in that state. So they changed the way it was consumed. From then on, red maize formed a substantial part of our basic ration. We were fed like animals. Bananas were no longer eaten when ripe; they had to be harvested green, then grated and dried to be mixed with rice.

In the collective kitchen, the grains of red maize that were kept for animals in the past were steeped in petrol tanks filled with water. They were steeped for at least a day and a night before being cooked over a wood fire in huge metal pots. The soaked maize was cooked from evening until lunchtime the next day, and then it was drained in huge baskets of woven bamboo. The maize was now ready for distribution. The cooks didn't keep enough wood for the fire during the rainy season, however, and even after being simmered for 10 to 15 hours the maize still wasn't cooked. The shells of the grains were very hard and the maize was indigestible; it could be seen all over the open air latrines.

The land in Kampong Cham is very fertile and the province is known for producing all kinds of produce such as fruit, vegetables, tobacco, maize, beans, sesame seeds, sweet potatoes, etc. It was in this region that the first rubber trees were planted around the year 1920, but in the past the peasants grew very little rice, preferring to trade for it rather than grow it themselves. They sold their garden produce to buy rice from neighbouring provinces like Kampong Thom where the people were called "the rice field people". The Old people of Kampong Cham were thus very surprised to see the Angkar impose the growing of rice, but exchanges between regions had become impossible, and each region had to become autonomous. The rice yield proved to be satisfactory nonetheless, but no matter how good the harvest was we still weren't given any extra food, and the main part of the harvest was transferred elsewhere by the Angkar.

The cooks boiled water in big pots in the kitchen, and everyone could help themselves freely; in fact water was the only thing we weren't deprived of. Before leaving for the fields every morning, however, we had to make sure we had enough drinking water to last us the whole day because, when the work was at its most intense, the leader had our meals carried to the worksite and we were unable to replenish our water supplies. If the day was longer than usual we'd run out of water and would be forced to drink from a canal or pond, using our scarf to filter the water.

In spite of the fact that the country had huge salt fields in the province of Kampot, salt had become a rare and precious commodity, so much so that we exchanged jewellery to get it. The Khmer Rouge didn't want to redistribute salt to the cooperative on the pretext that the Angkar had to export it. We were obliged to economise salt so the Angkar could export it, to the point where certain illnesses were caused by a lack of salt. At the same time, the salt production storehouses were saturated by their own production.

Sugar was even harder to get, but was often given as a special ration to increase our output on certain occasions. If we had to work extra hard, the cooperative gave us dessert. This was usually a very simple sugary soup made from a mix of sticky rice, green or black beans, maize, sugar, and with or without coconut milk. We thought this dessert was excellent and we loved it. Our leader asked us to thank the Angkar who had provided us this treat while or our brother and sister combatants of the second line forces didn't have this privilege. She thought the Angkar was some kind of god to be thanked at all times. We were often so exhausted that our bodies swelled up like a tire, and when someone suffered from swollen legs or arms, the cadres gave them two or three soup spoons of palm sugar as if it were medication. If we had nice cooks, they sometimes gave us one or two spoons of palm sugar without reproach and that eased us a little, but at other times the cooks criticised us, saying we were capitalists who had never worked hard. If we were ill, they called us bloodsuckers and said we lived off other people's blood. Palm sugar was a rare commodity for us, but it was shared openly amongst the Khmer Rouge cadres. Food was distributed in a hierarchical manner in a society that was supposed to be egalitarian; that was the real truth about the dictatorship of Democratic Kampuchea.

The province of Kampong Cham is also rich in fish, and each year the region produces tonnes of *prahok*, a sort of fish paste that the Khmer use in traditional dishes. During the dry seasons before 1975, hundreds of carts would come from neighbouring regions to get supplies of *prahok*. True to this tradition, the Khmer Rouge cadres sent all first and second line forces to prepare the paste as well as smoked, dried, and canned fish goods. We looked forward to this time of the year and knew we would be able to eat our fill of fish. We fished at night by the hundreds, and the next day we were busy cutting and preparing the fish, which we smoked on huge grills over wood and coconut charcoal. The fish was then made into a paste and we filled huge jars with it. Suddenly, we saw sacks of salt appear, but we'd been told there was a shortage so where had the sacks come from? We didn't dare ask. The work was hard and the hours were long, but the rations were better than usual, and we now had both rice and fish. Some of us couldn't stop eating until we got indigestion. We made fish balls, salt fish, or grilled fish and used the fish oils to light our nights. Each day we were knee deep in fish bits, and we collected all the leftovers from the cooking as well as the grease that floated to the surfaces of the pots. Finally the fishing was over, and the preparation of supplies was finished, but we stank of fish for up to a week afterwards. We loaded the supplies we had prepared onto carts for distribution, but we never saw the supplies again. Our rations were back to being as scarce as ever, and we went off to work on new jobs.

CHAPTER 7

KHMER COSTUME IN THIS NEW THEATRE

The net doesn't catch as many fish as ignorance catches fishermen.

Cambodian code of 1898

Costume has always been of major importance in our society, and traditional costumes are still worn today. Traditionally both men and women wore a sampot tied in the *kben* style; a simple sampot to the ankles; Chinese trousers; a long tube-like tunic; and a Chinese tunic. These clothes usually cover the body completely and help to protect the wearer from the hot sun, but the costume is also an important aspect of social, cultural, and even religious distinction. Colour also plays an important role in Khmer costume, and black was not traditionally favoured by Khmer people. Our ancestors believed black was unhealthy because it conceals dirt and is said to bring bad luck, and wedding guests are strictly forbidden from wearing black. Furthermore, Cambodian brides and grooms never wear white as they do in Europe, because white is the traditional colour of mourning. Bright colours are thus of the utmost importance in Cambodian wedding ceremonies, and the bride and groom undergo several colourful wardrobe changes.

Thread has not always been in plentiful supply in Cambodia, however, and to this day you sometimes hear old people using the Khmer expressions "*sleak-peang*", "*sleak-paaut*" or "*sleak-phteas*" which mean to wear the jar, the bucket, or the house, respectively, as one would wear a piece of clothing. These expressions refer to the shortages of clothing and fabric during World War II when the Japanese occupied the country and requisitioned thread for their war efforts. In some of the most remote areas, the peasants had only one proper set of clothes per family. If a visitor came to the house, one member of the family would wear the costume to receive the caller while the others hid their nakedness inside the house or behind jars or buckets. Cambodia opened up to imports when the war finally ended, and people from Phnom Penh were very much taken by French fashions. They wore a shirt with a collar and French trousers, pyjamas, dresses, pullovers, and Bermuda shorts, all of which they got by mail order from Europe. Clothing also varied during the prosperous period which followed our independence from France in 1953, and some Cambodians began to copy Thai, Malay, Chinese, or Vietnamese fashions. All throughout this period, however, clothing remained less plentiful for the lower classes, and manual workers, peasants, and blue-collar workers wore trousers, the *sampot*, shirts, and sarongs in dark colours. The *krama*, on the other hand, is a universal accessory and has always been used by both city dwellers and the rural population as a piece of clothing, a wrapping, a towel, a scarf, a bathing suit, a hammock for a baby, or for protecting one's head from the sun. It is often said the Khmer couldn't live without the *krama*, and it was the only piece of Khmer clothing retained under the Angkar. It formed an essential part of the Khmer Rouge combatants' uniform but, in spite of its many uses, the *krama* is a very ordinary garment. Nevertheless, because it was permitted by the Khmer Rouge, it took on great significance during the Angkar's regime and became a fashionable accessory like a scarf. All the girls tried to have a pretty *krama*, and young people asked their parents for them. The Angkar cadres were almost always young and couldn't hide their vanity, with some of the upper cadres even wearing silk *krama*. The two ends of the garment are usually decorated by little multicoloured hooks, but most of us New girls didn't even have a simple undecorated one. Even so, I was lucky enough to receive a present of an old red and white striped *krama* which I kept for important events, and I had an old piece of fabric which I used for everyday work.

Despite the relevance of the *krama*, the rest of the clothing profession disappeared entirely from the country. Centuries of clothing traditions vanished within a matter of months, and clothing styles were dramatically simplified. Our clothes were no longer reflective of our personalities, and dressing was stripped of any pleasure. Clothing was nothing more than a functional accessory of the fighter and worker, and everyone—Angkar cadres included—had to wear dark or black clothes. It is quite probable that the first soldiers' outfits imported from China were black, and this colour was then imposed by the Angkar as collectivist standardisation. Each person now possessed no more than two outfits and only one *krama*. The *sampot* was reserved for women on certain occasions, but all other traditional Khmer clothes were abolished. Both men and women now wore wide elasticated trousers and long or short sleeved shirts, with or without a collar. Despite this imposed uniformity, however, the need to add a personal touch to our clothes remained somewhat timidly, especially among us women. We wore anything that might be perceived as a sign of vanity beneath our uniforms and added personal touches to our undergarments to lift our spirits.

When I was 12 years old my mother had taught me to sew and knit, and this was something none of the other girls in my *korngchalat* knew how to do. I wasn't raised to be idle, and even though I worked in the fields during the daytime, I also worked at night to earn a little extra food. I'm convinced I would never have survived if I hadn't been able to sew because I had no family to help me or give me extra food. Often the *korngchalat* leaders asked me to make garments for them such as shirts, underclothing, trousers, and hats, and I spent many nights sewing under an oil lamp. Among the female cadres, who had more freedom than the rest of us, clothing accessories were replaced by other things, after fashions which surprised me. Sometimes they asked me to undo a pullover or a sweater in order to knit a cover for a radio, a lighter, or a lamp. One day a female leader of a *korngchalat* of 360 girls, Mitt Saun, who was built like a man and spoke with an assertive and authoritarian tone, came to me and ordered covers for a radio, as well as knitted and crocheted undergarments. She loved brightly coloured garments in red, blue, and green, and asked me to knit her clothes she knew she wouldn't be able to wear but which she could, at the very least, look at. Because we weren't allowed to wear jewellery, lamps and lighters had become objects of vanity for the cadres, as had novelty underwear. These were rare items which the cadres kept discreetly, but because the lamps and lighters served a useful purpose, the cadres could possess them legitimately. The oil in the lamps was now worth more than the most expensive perfumes, and the cadres placed covers on these objects with a gold or silver chain tied to the edge. They took out their lamps during each evening meeting, and it was obvious that this was more to make themselves shine than to light their way.

Lace bodices that city women used to wear during various traditional and official ceremonies were also very much in demand among the female cadres. They didn't wear them often and asked me to cut them up to make cups for their bras. They entrusted me to maintain and brighten up their underclothes, and shared needles, thread, and other accessories with me. Since the 1960s, the Khmer really liked the French Montaigut brand polo-shirts, and these were also in demand by the Angkar cadres. They didn't dare wear them during the day because this would have been seen as a sign of vanity of the former bourgeoisie, but they wore them at night. They wore the Montaigut polo-shirt under their black shirt, leaving the collar open a little to show it off. While we could have no further interest in our appearance, the cadres could, and the height of fashion for a Khmer Rouge cadre under Democratic Kampuchea was to have a red-striped krama, a black uniform, a Montaigut polo shirt, an Orient brand watch, and Ho Chi Minh sandals. For New girls like me, being fashionable was of no real concern. We had only one desire: to find enough food to survive. Every one of us prayed to Buddha and the spirits to keep us alive, and we would have done anything to be liberated from our borderless prison.

There was only one tailor available in the cooperative, and he was charged with making black uniforms for the entire community. Ta Oul, head of the cooperative and older brother of Yeay Pheap, called on me to help the tailor along with a few other girls. A former seamstress cut the fabric while three of us did the sewing with machines confiscated from the villagers. As well as making uniforms, we also received special orders from leaders of the various units, but I took advantage of my time to lengthen the sleeves of my two shirts and to position myself as near as I could to the collective kitchen. The food stocks were stored in the collective kitchen, and those who worked around the cooperative had a better chance of getting extra food. This meant I could get rice, crusts, and other leftovers to help appease my hunger. I heard from some of the other girls that special arrangements were made between the cooperative chief and some New families, whereby the family exchanged certain items to ensure them a good place in the cooperative. I had nothing whatsoever to give, but my experience in dress-making served me well, and I became well-known throughout the local men's and women's camps for another speciality: making hats from sugar-palm leaves.

I got orders for hats from all kinds of camp members and sometimes from higher level cadres, even from the president of the regional *korngchalat*. The members of the various camps placed their orders with me and gave me fruit or other food supplies in return. Making a hat from sugar-palm leaves is a tricky job, however. During the first stage you have to take the young Palmyrah palm leaves and dry them in the sun for two or three days. Once dry, the leaves can be cut into small regular strips with a traditional tool. The next step is plaiting the strips, and I took advantage of the criticism meetings to do this job. To make a woman's hat I needed more than 18 m of plaited sugar-palm leaves, and a bit less for a man's hat. These hats had become an essential accessory to cope with the hot sun on the work sites which functioned like giant anthills and never let up.

Despite the harshness of our living conditions, the desire to look after our bodies remained, and this was especially true in the case of the female cadres. The gap between the urban and rural populations in terms of living standards (which was reinforced by the outbreak of war in 1970) was immense, and the signs of poverty and poor hygiene could be seen on the Old girls' much-abused bodies. Years before, peasants used to wash themselves and their clothes with a liquid detergent made from *pti* plants, banana skins, and dried kapok shells. Pieces of soap were much rarer and were reserved for washing the hair and body. Now, nearly a century later, we had returned to these practices. Many of the girls didn't know how to wash themselves properly and most had no idea of the rules of hygiene. Some of them questioned me on facial care or asked me to pluck their eyebrows, and I did my best with what few resources were available to us.

Several of the girls talked openly to me, and I learned that a few of them had gone to school for two or three years and could read a little, but many others were illiterate. It was clear, however, that nothing was being planned by the new administration to fill the gaps in the education system. The population of the provinces lived from one generation to the next by reproducing the same habits and way of life as their parents. When would this change? It was obvious this new regime had abandoned education entirely, and I wondered what would become of the children who were not only cut off from school, but were now also cut off from their parents. How would they learn to look after themselves?

One day a *korngchalat* leader named Srean came to me and asked me to cut her hair. Laughingly, she added that if I didn't know how to do it, I'd be killed. I'd seen these threats carried out by Khmer Rouge cadres all too often, and I took the threat seriously. I was scared and had no idea what to do, but I didn't dare refuse. I had never cut anyone's hair before, but I knew that if I made myself useful I wouldn't be killed. She wanted a short pageboy cut that came to just below the ears, and I told myself it shouldn't be too difficult. Srean handed me a pair of scissors and a comb, and I did as I was told. I tried to remember the delicate movements of my mother's hairdresser back in Siem Reap. I took a deep breath, and divided her hair into two layers with the comb. Then I took the scissors and started cutting the bottom layer before I moved on to cut the top layer. Her hair was beautifully thick and the cut seemed to work. For the moment at least I was saved. Srean even complimented me, and after that first test I became the camp hairdresser.

The cut was always the same—a short pageboy—and I cut all the girls' hair in my *korngchalat*. Often the girls had hundreds of lice in their hair. After a few weeks of my new double life—front line labourer in the fields on some days and camp hairdresser on others—I developed painful calluses on my fingers. But I had given back a little femininity to girls subjected to forced labour and gloomy standardisation, and I was happy with my efforts.

This double life didn't last long, however, and soon made trouble for me. When I had to stay and work in the huts I obviously couldn't go to the works with the other members of the *korngchalat*, and some of the girls were jealous of me. The same reasons were always given: I was part of the capitalist class or the exploiters of the previous regime which was why I was working in the shade. The leaders of the camp paid attention to these criticisms and stopped giving me extra work except for two or three days a month. So I returned to work on the sites once more, but I started to think I was only being kept alive because of the services I provided to the cadres. I knew that if I stopped being useful they would easily do away with me, so I tried to work diligently in the fields and not draw too much attention to myself. But jealousy and even hatred had started spreading amongst us, and the Old girls paid close attention to my every move.

I felt the women were less tolerant than the men, and that they never stopped criticising: she's less of a worker; she's weaker than the rest of us; she's too fragile, etc., and quite often the targets were the best-looking girls amongst us. It was as if the criticism sessions had become not only a duty but a survival reflex and, the more difficult life became, the more the girls in the *korngchalat* spied on each other. I was very careful not to tell any of them, not even my friends, about my background. Some weren't fooled, however, and they kept a close eye on me, constantly fishing for information, but I preferred to say nothing at all to them so as not to compromise myself.

Srean was promoted in 1978 to replace comrade Saun who was single and had been caught with a man. She quivered at the idea of her new responsibility and gave me writing and calculation jobs to do for her. She appointed me to write up her own biography as well as the biographies of all the members of the *korngchalat* who couldn't write. From time to time she also had me write up various work reports for our camp and statistics for the chain of command. During meetings with the Angkar *loeu* hierarchy, Srean's work was praised for being well done, simple, and clear. She was complimented by her bosses and colleagues, but once or twice she was asked to do small extra jobs by herself and they noticed her handwriting was different, or that the content didn't correspond to her previous reports. She was terrified.

They knew she was getting help, and she was forced to admit that it was me who was helping her. The upper cadres interrogated her about my background, but she assured them I was the adoptive daughter of Ta Chourp and Yeay Pheap, and she said she didn't know my parents. They could easily have sent her for further questioning, but her superior, Comrade Ouk, and some of the other leaders, found her to be more efficient than *mitt* Saun whom she'd replaced. They also noted that she was hard-working and obedient, and the incident had no further consequences for either of us. The fact that she had given responsibilities to someone who was supposedly illiterate probably led the hierarchy to be more lenient, but at the time I had no idea any of this was going on. Srean couldn't tell me about being questioned, and it wasn't until afterwards that I learned about the interrogation. Certainly the leaders were occasionally nicer to me because they wanted to take advantage of my domestic or writing skills, but I was still a New person of 1975, and a traitor in the eyes of the Angkar. My life was worth nothing to them.

CHAPTER 8

RABBIT DROPPINGS CURE ALL

You can live in a narrow house but you can't live with a tight heart.

Khmer proverb

There was no escaping illness under Democratic Kampuchea, and from time to time on the work sites, we saw girls lying down in exhaustion, trembling, shivering, and sometimes fainting. The only cure for malaria was a concoction made from the bark of the Neem Tree, which contains fever-reducing quinine, and at least 10 girls in my *korngchalat* had malaria. Other girls experienced *sreut*, a neurovegetative illness, and dystonia, a neurological movement disorder, both of which are common in the Kampong Cham region. Those suffering from *sreut* or dystonia would get convulsions and lose consciousness. Because of our malnutrition, overwork, and anxiety, several of us weren't menstruating any more. Yet many of the girls saw this as an advantage and, since none of us were thinking of having a family, it was simply one less thing to worry about. Those who were seriously ill were sent to a regional hospital, but the doctors and nurses of Democratic Kampuchea were in fact young soldiers or the children of cadres who had been sent to the hospitals after the fall of Phnom Penh. They were given only a few months training by the handful of older doctors that remained among the Khmer Rouge, and we were told that theory and university degrees weren't important—only practice counted. There was practically no treatment or medication at the hospital, and most of the so-called doctors or nurses couldn't read or write Khmer properly. The hospital was nothing more than a rest-home.

In 1977 I fell ill, and on the written orders of our leader I was allowed to have myself cared for in the provincial hospital reserved for members of the front line force. This was the *damban* 41 hospital in Prey Chhor[1], the hospital of region 41. The leader considered this permission to be quite a nice gift, and I was given the privilege of experiencing the new medical profession's hospitality first-hand. The hospital reminded me of the *korngchalat* and, in each building, two rows of beds were lined up to receive the sick. I was having episodes of tetany and was suffering from *sreut*, but my friend Nany was also ill and was hospitalised in the same place. Luckily we were neighbours.

---

1   Today this is the hospital of Chrey Vean and has changed little in 30 years.

A few hours after I arrived, two nurses came to get information on my section and my biography. They told me the doctor's round wasn't planned until the following morning, and I would have to wait until then to be seen. During the night, one of the girls in a nearby bed was delirious and clearly dying. She rambled constantly, and the whole dormitory rang with sighs, groans, and tears from its various inmates. I couldn't sleep even though I was incredibly tired, and I felt very uneasy all that night. The next day, a young man between 25 and 30, wearing a grubby white coat—whom everyone called *mitt borng*, "comrade brother"—arrived to complete his round. He was accompanied by two nurses and, armed with a stethoscope, began to examine the patients one after another while the nurses distributed tablets from Angkar pharmaceutical labs. The tablets were about the size of a big grain of pepper and were black, yellow, or white. They were dispensed in any and every combination and were given to treat all ills, including *sreut*, malaria, fever, diarrhoea, etc., but in reality they were no more effective than the rabbit droppings dispensed by the nurse back in the cooperative.

Other liquid cures made in the same labs were kept in big serum bottles, and the nurses gave them to patients in the form of a tonic, an injection, or even a drip. They also gave drips of clear coconut water from freshly picked fruit, and after being given a drip of this liquid which was supposed to cure everything, several patients showed fresh symptoms or a new disease. Many developed abscesses where the drip or injection had been inserted, and this meant a longer hospital stay and further treatment. It was not a good idea to remain in hospital for very long. If the doctors and nurses didn't treat you to death, the Angkar authorities would begin to look at you as a usurper, and they wouldn't feed those who weren't productive. As the Angkar said, "Those who pretend to be ill are victims of their own imagination." The hospital used several methods to get rid of patients: they either progressively reduced their food ration to kill them slowly, or they simply selected patients to be sent back to their camps. The only advantage of the hospital was escaping from work for a while, but even then we didn't escape it completely.

During our hospital stay, all patients had to participate in the production of compost. Every morning we had to cut *kan-treang-khèt* herbs and chop them into a ditch to prepare natural fertiliser. We had the afternoons to ourselves, however, and the most able-bodied among us were able to hunt the surrounding area for potatoes, leaves, roots, fruits, insects, or little crabs to ease our hunger. Every day we got a ladle of soup, and sometimes it was mixed with maize or green bananas, but quite often it was reduced to a few grains of rice steeped in a clear soup, to the point where you could see the bottom of the aluminium bowl.

The atmosphere in the hospital was terrifying. I could constantly hear patients howling in pain, and thin bodies covered with bruises and ulcers were strewn about the place amid clouds of flies. More and more dead people were removed every day, and people defecated all over the place. The patients were exhausted, and the situation in which they found themselves had relieved them of all dignity; they no longer cared about hygiene. Not far from us the so-called nurses and doctors of the Angkar were well-fed and healthy looking, living even better than the Old people.

Traditional medicine had always been practised by the Khmer people, but it was more common in the rural areas than the cities where many doctors were trained abroad. Yet having been deprived of all modern medicines, and made to suffer the Angkar's cures, we soon returned to traditional medicine and began hunting for plant remedies. We went to see traditional doctors, the *krous*, who made potions, creams, unguents, ointments, fumigators, and plasters from various plants. Concoctions were made to treat several diseases, especially diarrhoea, stomach pains, internal and external infections, transmissible diseases, and so on. The Old people also prepared unguents made from plants or crushed roots, which they mixed with animal organs, bile, stomach juices, and crushed horns.

Each illness had its cure. An open wound was heated on a fire to ease the pain and to sterilise it. Blisters on the hand or foot were pierced with a toothpick or the stalk of a coconut leaf sterilised over a flame, so we could return to work. To treat a stomach ache we ran to the guava tree, whispered *op-kech*—a traditional guru formula—before gathering four or five young guava leaves to chew. Swollen neck glands were a common complaint because we had to carry heavy objects on our heads for hours, and to treat this we applied saliva collected upon waking in the morning, before we had cleaned our teeth, while saying the same prayer as before. For a crick in the neck, we put our pillows outside in the sun, while to dissolve kidney stones, we ate pineapples and drank a special brew made from pineapple roots and several other plants. For a swollen body, or to treat muscular cramps, sugar was prescribed. For burns, we took a crushed cactus and applied it to the spot to cool the burn. We then asked the guru to ease the fire poison before laying green banana leaves on the wound to stop the burnt skin from drying up. For a toothache, we chewed grains of salt, or put a few grains of monosodium glutamate on the painful tooth. For fever or dizziness, we made *kos-kchol*, which meant marking the chest or the arm with a coin or spoon to "hunt the pain", and I think that often the solidarity did more to improve our morale than the actual cures themselves. If sharing tasks and food often made us more independent and selfish, as living conditions continued to worsen, we were brought together by illness. Strangely, the Angkar tolerated this return to traditional medicine, as well as the presence of the gurus with their secular animist practices. Clearly the Organisation knew it had no other medical solution to offer us.

Four or five weeks into our hospital stay, Nany and I heard about a Chinese woman who could predict the future. We were so destitute that we were ready to rely on this soothsayer to reassure us. She didn't speak Khmer, but we tried to understand each other using sign-language. She told us that if we were to avoid danger, we should leave the hospital immediately and go back to our *korngchalat*. We thanked her with a few grains of salt, and resolved to leave as soon as possible.

CHAPTER 9

NEITHER MOTHERS NOR WIVES, WOMEN DON'T EXIST ANYMORE

Bunches of rice plants give life to the land, the woman gives life to the man.

Khmer proverb

Long ago, the kings of Angkor were influenced by the Hindu principles of the Indian caste system, and, originally, this division consisted of four main castes: the Brahmins were the highest caste, made up of priests and educated people—these were the holders of knowledge and rites; the *ksatriya* were the aristocrats and were generally nobles and warriors; the *vaicya* were craftsmen, merchants, or farmers; and finally, there were the *cudra*, who were workers or slaves. Before 1975, our society was regulated by a set of principles which had developed over centuries, and we believed we were each on an unchanging course determined by our karma. Each person's position in society was decided by accident of birth and kinship, and whether one was rich or poor, farmer or civil servant, in good health or bad, was determined even before our birth. This determinism could be hard to bear at times, but in a certain sense it protected us, and not having the choice to alter our destiny gave us a level of contentment.

The spread of Buddhism abolished the caste system, but Khmer society remained very hierarchical and was characterised by a strict separation of men and women. Male and female roles within the family unit were very distinct, as were their professional and social lives. The status of boys was different from that of girls, even from a very young age, and boys were granted a higher position in society than women. Intellectual work or hard labour belonged to boys, while girls were forced to leave school early. From the age of 10 or 12 onwards, Khmer girls learned how to keep house and be a good mother to their families. They had to help their mothers with household tasks and look after whatever little brothers or sisters they had, while the boys continued on through school and worked with their fathers or older brothers outside the home. In the country, boys helped their parents mind the animals, while in the towns they helped them transport goods. Household work, or the sale of garden produce, was strictly reserved for women. Money was held in common in the Khmer family, but the women looked after it, because they had to meet the household needs. This responsibility was often the source of rows and continuous conjugal violence among married couples, because, no matter what their behaviour was like, or what the cause of the bad luck in the household was, the men would often refuse to accept any blame if there wasn't enough money to meet the needs of the family.

Boys were believed to be protected by primeval spirits, and it was forbidden for women, young girls in particular, to cross over a boy's body, to touch a boy on the head, or to share their food with a boy. As the sayings go: "Do not touch the head of the boys; if you do, they cannot be soldiers," "You mustn't cross over a boy's body," "Girls don't dive deeply and don't go far either," and even, "Girls can't circumvent the kitchen."

The code of conduct for Cambodian women, the *Chbab Srey*, which set out the standards that women were expected to uphold, was part of the curriculum in both primary and secondary schools until very recently. The code tells the story of a married princess who had to follow her husband, while her mother-in-law gave her advice on how to be a good bride. The princess was taught to answer her husband with patience and understanding when he was angry, if he hit her, or if he had a mistress. She was told never to answer her husband back or be disrespectful to him. The princess's mother-in-law also told her that if she touched her husband's head without paying him the proper respects with joined hands, the *sam-peas*, she would experience bad luck in this life, and sin in the next. In a text dating from 1551, during the reign of King Preas Reach Ongkor, it was said that a queen must be "doted with all the favourable signs," and must observe the following five instructions: she must never sleep with anyone but the king; she must always wake up before the king; she must prepare him an excellent meal and give his orders to the slaves, so they always have something useful to do; she must always be full of respect for the king; and, finally, she must live in the shadow of the king, seeing him as her supreme master.

The *Chbab Srey* still influences the treatment of women in Cambodia today, though to a somewhat lesser extent than before, but the separation of the sexes was also due to the Buddhist religion, which kept women apart from monastic life and places of worship. While the pagodas welcomed and lodged young men, so they could conduct their studies in the nearby towns, girls weren't allowed to avail of this same accommodation. The number of girls accepted to the various educational establishments was always lower than the number of boys. There were plenty of girls in primary schools, somewhat fewer in secondary schools, and rarely any in the universities. The main reason for the persistently weak proportion of women in education, however, was the role given to women in the family, which prevented them from evolving or being emancipated from the home. If a family ever had need of extra help around the home, it was always up to the girls to give up their studies. This was the case when my father died, and it was suggested to my mother that I should stop going to school in order to help her around the house. But my mother didn't ask me to drop out, preferring to let me continue with my studies, which showed how much she favoured my freedom. My situation was an exception, however, and, in most cases, the cycle of the female role within Khmer society never progressed; it merely repeated itself from one generation to the next.

Khmer women had to belong to the same age group and the same generation as their husbands, but though they were similar in age, they were always somewhat younger. When a husband and wife addressed each other, they used generational terms such as *borng* (older brother) and *aunn* (little sister). In our culture, a man and woman had to be married if they wanted to live together, as cohabitation was frowned upon and left the woman in a very weak position. If a person wasn't married for life, it was believed that he or she had no predestined relationship, which is not in keeping with *dharma*, the Buddhist moral order. A woman who lived alone was called *kror-mom-sao-kè*, a derogatory expression used to describe a single woman beyond the age of 25 or 30, the age limit for marriage. It was said that such a woman was of loose morals, or she had some sort of defect and couldn't please a man. Single women had no recognised status; they didn't have the right to betel nut palm flowers, a symbol of bridal virginity which holds special significance in Khmer culture.

Marriage was encouraged and guided by family choices, and was almost always arranged. Whether or not two people consented to marry was considered insignificant; it didn't matter whether the future spouses had gotten to know one another properly, or to appreciate each other physically. My grandmother, for instance, had only seen my grandfather once before their marriage, and even then she only saw him from a distance. It was up to the parents of those to be married to propose the marriage between their children, and this was a prerequisite to reaching a successful union. In reality, the parents of a young man at an age to marry simply went looking for a young girl of equivalent social status, with a view to matrimony. A boy could sometimes choose a girl he liked and submit this choice to his parents, but the final decision lay with his parents. Tradition didn't permit the reverse, however, and girls had no say in the matter.

Thus, the various stages of marriage were as follows: the parents of a young man went looking for parents like themselves, preferably parents who were known in the village or surrounding areas, so they could be fully investigated. They then arranged a day to meet, and when that day arrived, the parents of the young man, accompanied by several members of their family, brought arec and betel, and a gift "to seek guidance on the path to take and the ladder to climb", together with fruit, cakes, and flowers. Their aim was to show the parents of the girl how well disposed they were and what resources they had. During this first interview, the dowry to be offered to the girl's parents was mentioned. This was called *khan-sla*, meaning offerings, and included the reimbursement of milk, the marriage charges, the engagement festival fee, and, for some traditional people, a trial period. Normally, the young man in question was not present at these negotiations, and an old tradition demanded that the young man be tested to prove his worth by living and working in the girl's family, where he assumed the role of servant[1]. This trial period formed the engagement,

---

1   This is the *nov-bam-roeu* tradition. See Article 19 of Krâm Tous Pîriyea of 1853: "A man who, after requesting the hand of a girl in

which could last anywhere between six months and three years, allowing the girl's family to get to know the young man better, and to test his capacities, his behaviour, his conduct, and his patience. This period was truly a rite of ordeal, and the young man's potential in-laws would try very hard to test the limits of his skills. If he didn't perform successfully, he could be sent home, and the engagement would be broken off. The gifts that had been offered would not be returned, and the parents of the young man would lose face.

It could also happen that a marriage was negotiated years in advance between friends, with each party committing to marriage when their children grew up. In well-off families, marriage and property alliances were sometimes set up before the children were even born, as is common in India. Well-off families didn't mark their girls out for boys of poor families, unless they showed serious professional potential and possessed good university degrees. A good career step for a lower middle-class Cambodian man, therefore, was to marry a girl from a good family. In traditional practice, a young man had to do a training course in a Buddhist monastery, where he acquired his initial education, and, if he was talented, he could draw the attention of influential members of the community. The gifted young man thus started his social climb by marrying the daughter of a property

---

marriage and offering the *khan-sla*, arec and betel to the girl's parents, with their consent and that of his own father and mother, lives for two or three years with the girl's parents, serving them, earning his living with them, is, in the eyes of the law, the lawful wedded husband of that girl, even though the wedding meal has not yet taken place."

owner, a tradesperson, a high-ranking civil servant, or a government official. He could then use his wife's money to complete his studies, settle down, cover his needs, and get a good job. If the difference in class was too wide, the parents of the girl might refuse to receive the young man. A woman from a poor family had no means of climbing the social ladder, because she was judged on her lineage, not on her merits. Marriage was conducted like a business transaction. It was presented as the merger of a woman's hereditary capital, with a man's education-based assets.

When it came to the ceremony itself, the two families consulted an *achar*, a guru, or a bonze to find the most favourable day for the wedding. The guru or bonze made a prediction based on the birth dates of the couple, in order to ascertain the most favourable date. Once the date was set, the bride's family received all the guests, including those of the groom. The groom's family relied on a master of ceremonies, called *chao-moha*, who was honourably known in the village, to play the role of negotiator on their behalf. In the country, they brought the bride's family food supplies such as live pigs, live cattle, rice, glutinous rice, green beans, cakes, and sesame seeds. Being a superstitious people, the Khmer did everything to ensure that the new couple were both "in the intimate peace and calm where two souls abide," as tradition required. Whatever the circumstances, it was only after the marriage had actually taken place, and when the couple had lived together for some time, that love could perhaps awaken between them; in many cases they grew to be close.

This picture of family and social organisation puts in context a time when it was turned upside down by a new authoritarian order. All of our traditions were forbidden, and what had been our culture and way of life was sacrificed for a utopia imposed by the Khmer Rouge. We were forced to endure a level of brutality that hadn't been seen anywhere before, not even in the worst moments of the Chinese Cultural Revolution.

Democratic Kampuchea declared the respect of the rights of women and the equality of both sexes. The Constitution of Democratic Kampuchea of 5 January 1976 stipulates in Article 13: "There must be complete equality among all Kampuchean people in an equal, just, democratic, harmonious, and happy society within the great national solidarity for defending and building the country together. Men and women are fully equal in every respect. Polygamy and polyandry are prohibited." In reality, the concept of the family unit was destroyed, and families were wiped out. The Angkar's so-called equality among all people, despite the obvious separation of the sexes, simply meant that all men or women, regardless of age or physical strength, were now forced to do the same hard labour equally. There was no longer any familial reference. The family structure was replaced by one great union of the entire Khmer people, under the protective authority of the Angkar. Under the Khmer Rouge regime, Khmer families were broken up, and individuals were regrouped according to their generation, sex, and marital status. Fathers now lived among other fathers, and mothers lived among other mothers. Unmarried children were separated according to their sex and sent to live with other unmarried boys or girls. Younger children were also separated from their families and sent to live with each other. Even grandfathers and grandmothers were separated. In some regions, the group divisions had certain distinctive characteristics, but the structure of the work regime was the same throughout the country. We only got together or saw one another in the evenings, and the members of the various *korngchalat* who were considered front line forces, rarely saw their families. In my *korngchalat*, the family reunion was only granted once during those four years. Those of us who were alone, had no reason to leave the camp except to carry out family research, but there was little point in that since the family didn't exist any more.

All the work was imposed, none of it was chosen, and the uniform dress reinforced the unisex nature of the work force: men and women were totally interchangeable, and everyone had to work. Only a few female cadres, or the wives of some well-known figures of the regime, were allowed to do office work. All other women shared the same manual jobs as men. In all the projects imposed by the Angkar, women were charged with carrying out the same tasks as men, like building dykes of 20 m per day, or digging trenches of 3 m^3 of earth per day to build a dam. Women worked everywhere, from the paddy fields, to the big sites for dam or road building. Even women of 70 or 80 years of age had to take part in rural works, in order to meet the programme of self-sufficiency implemented under Democratic Kampuchea. My grandmother, who was over 69 years of age at the time, also had to work. She was given "light" work, such as minding children or hunting animals in the paddy fields.

The Khmer Rouge deliberately turned family members against each other, by forcing them to struggle against the idea of family. They told us, "Don't trust the heavens any more, don't trust the stars, don't trust your daughter, and don't trust your mother." Children were promoted to the rank of militia, and they spied on their parents. The youngest members were called on to flush out "the new traitors of the nation" from among their parents. They were systematically taught to eliminate their elders, as older people couldn't be fully retrained or integrated into the new regime. The Khmer Rouge were very clear about splitting up families, effectively achieving their goal by leaning on the youngest and adopting parricidal practices. No one was safe in Democratic Kampuchea, not even from one's own children.

UNION BY COUPLE UNDER THE ANGKAR

The wind pushes the kite ahead of it.
Possessions grow because the woman who knows
how to look after them.
And the woman gaily pushes the family before her.
Proverb of the venerable Chuon Nat

In *damban* 41, and in the village of Phum Thmey where I lived, marriage was strictly controlled. The Angkar permitted marriage only between those Old people whom the Angkar considered sufficiently re-adapted and converted to the new regime. These people were referred to as "having reconstructed oneself well". The idea of marriage, as described earlier, had totally disappeared, and this union was no longer founded either on the civil law prior to 1975, or on Khmer tradition. The consent of future spouses or parents was no longer of use. No one had a say but the Angkar, and it was only under this authority that consent to marry was granted. New people like me constituted an inferior category which had no access to marriage.

The word "marriage" in the Khmer language, *rieap-kar*, or more literally, *rieap-a-pia-pi-pear*, was no longer used in Democratic Kampuchea. The Angkar invented a new expression, *rieap-krousar*, which can be translated as "arranging a family". According to the Khmer Rouge, the union of marriage was not meant to establish a family, but to produce "pure" children. We were told that those who were selected to be united were model young people, who had made a success of their retraining and their integration into the new society. In order to better supervise the population, and to combat individualism, the regime of Democratic Kampuchea periodically organised pairing ceremonies to unite between 10 and 50 couples at a time. The future brides and grooms didn't know each other before the ceremony, and most of them had never seen their future spouse. Only some superior Angkar cadres knew each other slightly before their marriage. Those men and women who were forced to unite, were only told that their name had been registered on a list of people to be married. They were then given a date for a marriage ceremony at which they had to attend. The Organisation was the sole master of all Cambodians living in Democratic Kampuchea, and we had to place our trust in the Angkar, who managed everything.

In most cases, the parents of those to be married weren't invited to attend the union of their children, because, as we were constantly reminded, their children were no longer theirs—they were children of the Angkar.

The two families were only introduced after the public ceremony, with the Organisation exercising parental authority in giving its consent to marriage. When the day for the ceremony arrived, the Angkar called a meeting of the cadres in charge of the groups to be married. The girls and boys lined up facing each other. Traditional costumes were no longer permitted, and the brides and grooms were each dressed in their black uniforms, wearing a *krama* and Ho Chi Minh sandals. If the parents had been informed, they were permitted to attend the marriage.

The ceremony began with a speech from a cadre of the highest rank, who spoke of building the country, of self-sufficiency, of the objective of three harvests of rice per year, of a yield of three tonnes per hectare, of the preservation of Khmer culture, etc. We wondered what culture the Angkar was trying to preserve since no memory of the past was permitted. When the cadre had finished his speech, another cadre called out the names of the men and women to be united, one after another. The future couples were invited to shake hands like communist comrades, showing that their marriage was an act of building a "new" society. At the end of the ceremony, a groom who had been designated specifically to represent all the couples, uttered a few words of thanks and gratitude to the Angkar for having taken care of them, and promised that the couples would each serve the Organisation faithfully to their dying day. Everyone clapped and the ceremony ended with a ringing "Long live the revolutionary Angkar." The new couples were now man and wife, and a meal that was more copious than usual was offered to them and their parents. Many of the parents cried secretly in their homes without saying a word about their despair. Certain families, in regions less strict than ours, were allowed to organise a little traditional ceremony in their homes to announce the marriage of their children to their ancestors. In our culture this is an essential gesture, because this announcement to the ancestors means getting their protection in return. But for those who had to remain silent, the abandoning of this ritual was viewed as a sign of malediction for the future.

The female cadres who were selected for marriage also had other concerns to face, because sometimes they were allotted a husband who had been disabled while serving as a soldier during the war. They were forced to sacrifice themselves to serve as wife and nurse to these veterans who were considered heroes of the revolution. Everyone owed gratitude to the Angkar, and the choice of husband was non-negotiable, whether they liked him or not. Before the marriage, the women cadres waited anxiously to see what their fate would be. They discussed it secretly among themselves, but their fears spread to us girls in the *korngchalat*. We heard that in other regions the Angkar had extended forced marriages to disabled soldiers to members of the *korngchalat* as well. We were terrorised. From then on, we covered our faces with our *krama* when we saw disabled soldiers pass by, for fear they might like the look of us.

One day in the *korngchalat*, we learned that one of our leaders had been designated for marriage. She was sent away to attend a pairing ceremony, and came back three days later with a disabled man who had lost a leg during the war. She pretended to be happy for fear of reprisal, but it was obvious that she was actually melancholic and sad. Sometimes I saw her and her new husband cycling together, and I didn't think she was enjoying the privilege of being the wife of a high level revolutionary. It didn't look to me as though their love would grow.

After the marriage ceremony, the new couples were given three or four days off. Their rooms were prepared for them, and in each there was a mat, two pillows, and a blanket. When night fell, the Angkar militia kept careful watch outside the rooms to make sure the marriages were consummated. As the Angkar said, "The walls have ears even at night." If the militia found that anything was wrong, meaning a marriage wasn't consummated, the couple in question were open to sanction. Those who contested the Angkar's forced coupling were sent to retraining centres, or to different cooperatives where the work was harder, the food was scarcer, and sanitary conditions were worse.

Another objective appeared clearly in the plan for revolutionary cleansing under Pol Pot's regime. This was the selection and forced procreation of "pure" people according to specific criteria, which calls to mind Hitler's fascist regime. The regime selected certain human beings it considered worthy or successfully retrained, to reproduce and help carry out its plan for an ideal society. Following this logic, one can see why the Angkar dismissed certain groups it considered socially impure.

Women were completely exploited by the Angkar authorities, and love and affection no longer had any value. Women were reduced to objects and slaves. If a man had sufficient hierarchical ranking, he could ask the Angkar to give him any woman he wanted, and the consent of the girl or her parents was no longer requested. She had to accept whatever she was offered, for fear of reprisal. This situation severely weakened relations in a couple, and many women, despite their efforts, had children from forced marriages. Nevertheless, they secretly hoped to get their freedom back[1], and bided their time.

In our region, New people weren't permitted to get married among themselves, or to marry a man or woman who was one of the Old people. The difference between the two classes was made very distinct, and in other regions New people had to marry with New, while Old people had to marry with Old. After our liberation by the Vietnamese in 1979, I learned that the leader of the boys' *korngchalat* had requested the consent of the Angkar loeu to marry me, but the Angkar managers considered the fact that I was a woman of 17 April 1975 and wasn't yet sufficiently reconstructed. I also learned that throughout the various waves of purging, this man was murdered by the Khmer Rouge.

---

1   As a court judge in Siem Reap in the 1980s, I noticed that the number of divorces was very high and that most of them had been filed by women. This new situation was caused by the Angkar, because before 1975 it was mostly the husbands who filed for divorce.

I saw no other member of our *korngchalat*, whether widow, widower, or divorced person get permission to marry under the Khmer Rouge regime. In the same way, none of the Old people were granted permission to marry their children—every request was flatly refused. In the village, it was the village leader who authorised marriages. Only married people could live in the village as a family, and those who lived in the village had a freer and easier life than those who lived in the *korngchalat*. They received small privileges: the work imposed on the married people wasn't so hard, and the married people were less supervised than the *korngchalat*. After work, they could go home to sleep, they could grow plants and vegetables around their houses, steal a few ears of corn, a few bananas or rice crusts, secretly kill a chicken, catch crabs and fish in the rice fields, or collect leaves and roots in the woods. Because the village was considered the secondary battlefield and more in the background, the chances of surviving there were higher than in the *korngchalat*.

In the *korngchalat*, it was the leader of the mobile brigades of the entire region who possessed the power to grant permission to marry, but the practice varied from one village to another. It might happen that a village leader would ask single men or widowers to choose a woman they liked: this was the practice of *chap-arom*, which allowed a man to choose his spouse. Then he was granted permission to marry. The union happened in two stages, the selection by the man, followed by the union. Relations between men and women were severely supervised, however, and choosing a match was not easy. The members of the girls' *korngchalat* stayed with the girls, while the boys remained with the boys. We worked in the fields together during the day, but even then the separation of the sexes was very strict. The cadres watched us day and night, and the Angkar saw everything and knew everything. Monogamy was the official rule under the Khmer Rouge regime[2], and cohabitation, like polygamy, was a crime. Men and women who allowed their passion to be freely expressed, exposed themselves to severe punishment and even a death sentence.

It has to be emphasised that the administration under the Khmer Rouge regime wasn't centralised according to a single or identical pattern. It was, therefore, not unusual to notice regional differences. Orders were given out by the superior Organisation, but the procedures weren't written down, and it was left to the initiative of the leaders in each region to interpret them. After the fall of the Khmer Rouge regime, it was noted that in certain villages purging had been a lot less severe than in other places, and that some traditional customs had even been tolerated. This was a direct result of the political context of each region, combined with the personalities of the figures in power. In the same fashion, a majority of New people in a region might have actually played in the people's favour, as was the case in the province of Preah Vihear, where

---

2   Polygamy had previously been authorised by the 1967 Civil Code (Article 141 stipulates that men can marry several wives, while Article 140 stipulates that women can only marry one husband). The monogamy rule of Democratic Kampuchea was carried on by the People's Republic of Kampuchea, 1979-89.

there were far more New people than in Kampong Cham or Battambang. Even Lon Nol's army officers managed to survive in Preah Vihear.

At a central level, the cadres were more loyal and obedient to the Angkar than at a regional or local level. This was because the administration of the State was deployed through political and military figures, rather than State intermediaries. The higher regional cadres had plenty of autonomy and were not kept in check unless there was a significant doubt about their loyalty to the Angkar.

CHAPTER 11

THE EDUCATION OF CHILDREN

The Angkar doctrine was designed to reinforce collectivisation and to partition groups. The members of each team had to remain united, move around in a group, work, eat, and sleep together. The teams were never allowed to mix. The children of New people were referred to as "the children of 17 April", and the children of the Old people were called the "Old children".

The children of 17 April no longer lived with their parents, because, according to the Angkar, children didn't need a family. The Organisation became the mother of our children, and we had to hand them over to it without question. We had to trust the Angkar completely. It assumed all parental authority, and declared that children would have a special diet. They would get fruit, sugar, sweets, and cakes in its name. The Organisation would ensure their health because the future of the country lay with them. In spite of the Angkar's declarations, however, the children's food was no different from that of everyone else; their food ration was fixed by the *sahakor*. During the harvest, they were given plenty of rice, but a few weeks later, they would get only soup or rice with a few grains of maize or banana shoots, just like the adults. In 1978, even though the harvest was good, hunger and starvation became more and more of a problem. As soon as the crops were harvested, all the food supplies vanished. Like the adults, the children thought of nothing but feeding their hunger. Our starvation ate at us and could be seen in everyone's eyes and on everyone's face.

The cadres told us: "Children are like a blank page on which we can write anything the Angkar wishes. When they receive an Angkar education, they are serving the revolution. The parents have inscribed imperialist and revisionist ideas on their character so they may no longer ensure the education of their children." Any father who gave a slap or a spank to his own child risked capital punishment because he no longer possessed any parental authority over his children.

In order to strongly influence the abolition of parental authority, children were taught to call their parents *mitt*, meaning comrade, and many children did. Subjected to such indoctrination, with their only guidance now coming from the cadres, some children even went so far as to denounce their parents' position prior to 17 April 1975. Their parents didn't feed them, the Angkar did, and their loyalty to their families quickly dissolved. The Angkar was presented almost as a divine entity, and this false and deeply-feared organisation now decided each Khmer's fate, from childhood onwards.

I noticed that the children in the Angkar centres learned nothing of importance, and their education was often reduced to learning revolutionary songs. There was no school of knowledge for its own sake, and there were no school materials or books. I could probably have taught the children something, but this would have revealed my education and given me away. I didn't dare speak to them. My family were never far from my mind. I wondered how my mother was, and if my younger brothers and sisters were okay. There was no communication at all, no news from my family in Siemreap. The Angkar said when you live in one place, you need to know about yourself, not other people. That was exactly the way we proceeded in our day to day life. It was the only way to survive.

My youngest sister Naroat, who was six at the time and living in a children's centre in Siem Reap, later said she learned nothing at the Khmer Rouge school, where no one knew how to read or write, least of all the teacher. School was part of the past, and, from now on, only practice counted. Each child was attached to a team and was forced to work with that team. The team leader made them collect cow pats or cut grass, destroy termite mounds to make fertiliser, chase away birds that were eating seeds in the paddy fields, or help in the collective gardens. They had no toys to play with, and a plate and a spoon were the only things they possessed. Everything else belonged to the Angkar: the huts, the gardens, the tools, the land, the forests, the frogs, the snakes, and the field rats—absolutely everything. Nothing remained for us or for our children, and we were forced to work like animals for every morsel of food the Angkar gave us.

We often heard cries and tears coming from the children's centre. The little children were hungry or ill, and we could hear them fighting amongst themselves. They were often punished by their leaders for misbehaving, and punishments were carried out even on very young children. Naroat spoke of receiving revolutionary punishments in Siem Reap. She told me she was deprived of meals and hit on the back, while the other children were incited to hate her. The leader encouraged the whole team to throw her in the mud and into animal excrement. When parents went by the children's centre, their children's eyes followed them, but they didn't dare approach, being held back by fear.

The Angkar didn't keep people who weren't productive; everyone had to work, and there was no special status for children when it came to hard labour. The very young were given light jobs like collecting manure, watering gardens, and serving as scarecrows to keep birds away from the rice or crops, but they reached adult age as soon as they could carry the weight of a hoe or a weapon. Another of my sisters, Sophea, who was eight at the time, had to work like an adult. Each day she transplanted rice or filled in channels. If a local dam was in danger, she was sent along with the other children to carry bundles of hay to fill in the holes, with water reaching up to their necks.

The children's groups were the preferred workforce of the Khmer Rouge because they were docile and more malleable than adults. In the village of Phum Thmey where my *korngchalat* was stationed, children over 10 years of age were called on to serve in the various organisations of Democratic Kampuchea. They were divided up according to the Angkar's needs: some were sent into the army, others into the medical area, and so on. Children learned quickly, the cadres said. They explained that the first generation of cadres had failed, but that the second would be worth more.

Little by little, our innocent young children started behaving like wolves. They judged their parents and their aunts and uncles. In the dispensaries it was said that children were remarkably intelligent at giving nursing care. They were shown a red box containing vitamins or how to sterilise medical instruments, and imitation and authority replaced knowledge and know-how. Other children and teenagers were enrolled as soldiers, as was the case with Sambat, the youngest son of Ta Chourp and Yeay Pheap. He was 17 at the time, and from the moment he left to serve the Angkar *loeu*, his parents heard nothing more from him. They were simply told that Sambat was part of the *yothea*, the soldiers of the Angkar, and they would never even learn how he died. When I visited them in 1996 they told me that they had had no news of their son since the liberation on 7 January 1979 and that they were now convinced he was dead.

This practice of early conscription had been in place since 1970 and was enforced from the age of 12 in the "liberated" regions. Young people guaranteed greater docility and asked fewer questions, making them perfect to carry out the Angkar's orders. From 1975, the systematic enrolment of young people and children had begun to produce results. In every rank of the Khmer Rouge, we could see young soldiers swimming in their oversized *khoor-ao-khmao*, the famous black trousers and shirt. There was no longer any question of the Angkar's aim to reduce inequality. It was clear that the Organisation's real aim was to create an army of children by converting them into obedient little soldiers without any education.

This picture was taken of me at 15 years of age. Before the Khmer Rouge came to power, I was just a young student, an ordinary Cambodian, far removed from political movements which went unnoticed in my province of Battambang.

On 17th April 1975, a group of young soldiers came to the house. They announced that we had to leave the house immediately because the Americans were going to bomb the city in a short while. Phnom Penh emptied like a body losing blood.

My uncle's house in Phnom Penh was large and luxurious.

After the Khmer Rouge took power, they treated us worse than animals, putting us into communal houses and feeding us red maize, which had been used to feed animals in the past.

Building a dam (above and below). In all the projects imposed by the Angkar, women were charged with carrying out the same tasks as men. Ours was a prison universe, and our country had been turned into an open air prison.

Even old women and children had to work hard for the Khmer Rouge. Our lives were worth nothing to them, unless we were productive.

Left and bottom: Pictures from a wedding under the Khmer Rouge.

A rare picture of Pol Pot, one of the founders of the Khmer Rouge.

© Nelson Rand

In the past, it was up to parents to propose marriage between their children. Once the Khmer Rouge took control, the consent of spouses or parents was no longer of use. No one had a say but the Angkar.

Discipline was formidable. Whether it rained or whether we were sick or tired, we had to work like machines.

Here I am pictured (left) with the people who took care of me during the Khmer Rouge regime, Ta Chourp and Yeay Pheap. They were like my foster parents.

I became friends with some of the girls from my *korngchalat*. Here I am with Srean and Vanny in happier times, 28 years later.

CHAPTER 12

THE SOMBRE DESTINY OF BUDDHISM AND THE KHMER-ISLAM OR CHAM MINORITIES

Oh my precious pralung, *the place of salvation where you think you are at this moment is actually utter darkness, where some stick their tongues out and others make a knot to hang themselves.*
The calling of the souls, Khmer ritual poem

In the past, our national religion had accompanied all of life's big events: festivals, marriages, deaths, and so on. However, Buddhism was completely abolished a few months after the fall of Phnom Penh in 1975. The regime's plan was to rid the country of Buddhism, even though Article 20 of the Constitution of Democratic Kampuchea, stipulated that each citizen had the right to his own beliefs and his own religion. In reality, however, and in conformity with Marxist-Leninist ideology, every reactionary religion was forbidden because it threatened the people of Democratic Kampuchea. The 3,000 pagodas erected all over the country were put out of use, and the 68,000 bonzes of the two orders, *mohanikay* and *thommayut*, were forced to give up their vows, leave their pagodas, don the black shirt of the peasant, and live from their work in the paddy fields. All this was designed to illustrate that religion was of no use and to break our morale. In my district of Korng Meas, the bonzes quickly disappeared from the pagodas, and the population were now afraid to approach the buildings, fearing them to be haunted by errant souls.

The Pol Pot regime re-established the warrior spirit and promoted the superior caste of Angkar combatants, for whom all of the regime's privileges were reserved. The New people were viewed as pariahs in the Hindu sense, and were placed at the lowest level of the social ladder, cut off from the Buddhist principles of equality. Was it deliberate that the Khmer Rouge tolerated some Brahmins in order to accommodate the spirits and the fury of the gods? I often wondered. Buddhism had certainly become invisible, but it still existed in our hearts and provided a spiritual therapy against our pain. Our religion invited us to resign ourselves to our fate because nothing could change our *karma*.

The Khmer Rouge transformed the pagodas into prisons, interrogation and torture centres, or into agricultural premises, rice granaries, or piggeries. The Monisaravorn pagoda, Wat O Trakuon, one of the ancient pagodas in the Prek Kror-bao commune, was converted into the main prison of the Korng Meas district and remained so until 1979. The building at the Buddhist monastery in Preah Vihara, a place of prayer sacred to bonzes and Buddhists, where the austere ceremonies of the Theravada school of Buddhism were held, was transformed into a huge communal cell for the internment of New people from 1973 and 1975. The victims were handcuffed and chained side by side—as one would chain cattle—to a metal bar attached to the walls on either side of the building. An old primary school next to the pagoda was also transformed into an interrogation room. The prisoners were executed in this building and then buried in the sacred pools within the pagoda enclosure. Iron handcuffs, pulleys, and other objects of torture, were discovered along with blood stains right after the departure of the Khmer Rouge in 1979. Reports established by the executioners of this prison, counted 38,690 victims who lost their life there. We learned that this was the final destination of all those men and women we had seen disappear from our ranks, month after month. The choice of sacred places to carry out such awful atrocities could have had only one motive; that of deconsecrating them and humiliating those who served them, because other buildings in the commune could have been used for the same purpose.

Chhom Phirun and her husband, inhabitants of the village, recall that at the moment of the executions, the members of the San-tek-sok, the political police, covered the howling, tears, and cries of their victims with music, but that the inhabitants of the surrounding villages could still hear them. Muy Vanny, another inhabitant of the village, was nine years old at the time and served as one of the little messengers of the chief of police of Wat O Trakuon. She remembers the victims supervised by the militia walked normally when going to an interrogation, but stumbled in pain when coming back.

In all the places we frequented, the statues of the Buddha had been systematically destroyed by Angkar members and the Khmer Rouge. It was not only a question of eliminating the clergy, but also all the fundamental representations of Buddhism, in order to prevent any direct devotion to the Buddha. Some of the most venerated divinities of the country were also destroyed, such as the two sisters Preah Ang Chek & Preah Ang Chorm, who had held pride of place over the Royal Square in Siem Reap. Their statues were ostentatiously thrown in the river. "The bonzes are parasites: prostrating oneself before the Buddha is like prostrating oneself before cement," we were told. The pagoda, as both a place of social gathering and the site of an opposing force, created many obstacles and brakes for the revolutionary order.

There was no trace either of the *neak-ta* places of worship. The earth-protecting spirits from the region, the province, the village, the hearth, and the water were no longer credited with supernatural powers. We New people were a displaced population: to which *neak-ta* could we make an offering, when we had nothing personal to offer? We no longer had any point of reference. The family household had disappeared, and the village was nothing more than a way-station, a place that was cursed because its protecting spirits had deserted it.

In my *korngchalat*, there were ten girls from the Cham minority. The Khmer-Islam people, to whom they belonged, were descendants of a great empire, the

Champa, which had stretched along the east coast of Indochina. In the 12th century AD, the Cham, who were both rich and powerful, fought a series of wars with the Angkorian Khmer, but were ultimately defeated by King Jayavarman VII. From the 15th century onwards the empire of Champa was systematically wiped out due to Vietnamese expansion, and King Pô Chien, the last Muslim Champa king, fled to Cambodia with many of his people. Despite our history of fighting against the Cham, they were welcomed by the Khmer and settled in the region known as Kampong Cham. They became loyal subjects of the king of Cambodia, but retained their language, customs, and Muslim religion. They peopled the banks of the Mekong and lived from activities related to the river.

From the first day they joined the camp, the Khmer-Islam girls were separated and prevented from speaking their language. They were obliged to abandon their headscarves and eat the same dishes as the Khmer, because the Khmer Rouge insisted that we were all equal and no differences would be tolerated. They didn't find it easy to share their lives with us Khmer girls, and they suffered greatly from it. In the beginning, some of the girls resisted and only pretended to eat pork when it formed part of their ration. But our leaders insisted, and finally forced them to sacrifice their traditions under pain of exclusion and imprisonment. They had difficulty integrating into the community of Khmer girls and often kept to themselves, which the leaders couldn't tolerate. The Cham were despised by the Khmer Rouge and were often singled out for execution in many regions. At the end of the Khmer Rouge regime, there were only four or five Cham girls left in our camp, even though they had been classified as Old people because of their rural origins. The historian Ben Kiernan counts 250,000 Cham before the civil war and estimates that only 173,000 survived. Elizabeth Becker on the other hand reckons that half of the Cham were massacred under the Khmer Rouge regime.

I would learn later from Srean, the camp leader, that the Cham girls were actually spared more than us New people, because they hadn't visited their families at the time of the great purges in 1978. The militia spied on us during these family visits in order to ensure they eliminated all the members of our families. Their families were pursued in their original villages and were the preferred targets of the political police, but they were relatively protected in our *korngchalat*, and some of them managed to survive.

In 2007 I visited Wat O Trakuon, and Mr Tay Kim Hé, an inhabitant of the village, admitted to me that the Angkar had put him in charge of transporting the Cham families from all the nearby villages by cattle wagon to the militia installed in the pagoda. As soon as the wagons arrived, the militia took the adults and children to be executed, at a rate of about twenty per day. Most of the Khmer-Islam from the Korng Meas district were wiped out here, in this pagoda. Kim Touch remembers one Cham family of six people, two parents and four children, who lived beside her. One day this family abandoned their home, even though it was forbidden to move. The Old people said they were tracked down, taken away during their meal, and killed. Mr Thov Chou, an inhabitant of another village near the same pagoda, believes that the massive elimination of the Cham was concentrated towards the end of 1978. The elimination of Vietnamese citizens, whom the Khmer Rouge believed might serve as relay to the Vietnamese army, also happened at the same time. We later learned that this was what is called genocide.

The Khmer Rouge would execute the parents first, while the children remained behind in their camp. They would then bring along the children, and when they couldn't find their parents, they in turn were executed. In early 1978, Nga, a New 17 April girl, joined us. Her father had been a primary school teacher in Phum Thmey. For once, our leader had received permission from the Angkar *loeu* to give us three days off to visit our families; in my case, this meant Ta Chourp and Yeay Pheap. Nga and I both lived in Phum Thmey, and we were so happy to get out at last. When Nga arrived in the village around midday, she could find neither her parents, nor her brothers and sisters. She was distraught and cried, and that same afternoon she was taken away by the militia and killed not far from the village. When Ta Chourp and Yeay Pheap heard this, they asked me to return quickly to my *korngchalat*. I was really frightened and left the following morning at dawn. The barbarity of this genocidal practice corresponded to the Khmer Rouge motto: "Once you've cut down the tree, you have to destroy the young shoots."

In the daily life of the *korngchalat*, if one of the girls did something wrong, the cadres would sneer at her, laughing: "You'll be sent there," meaning to the nearby pagoda which had been transformed into a place of murder. Death was by our side at the end of each day—never visible but always feared. We believed we were the result of our past actions, and this principle incited us to resignation: why revolt when what we were experiencing was the product of our own *karma*? To revolt would have been suicidal. But I knew I had to resist in silence. Modesty was the weapon of the weak, and only my determination would win out against their violence.

ANGKAR FESTIVALS AND THE MUTILATION OF THE KHMER LANGUAGE

Every day of work is a day of celebration.
Khmer Rouge motto

"*Tha-ngay na kor bonn*" means "Every day is a day of celebration," but we could never manage to accept this idealistic vision from the past in our current wretched state. When a day of official rest arrived, for us it was simply a day to recover our strength. In the camp, we didn't have to work, and everyone received a more copious meal than usual, followed by a dessert. The *sahakor* procured more provisions on these special occasions, and we saw pork or beef suddenly appear, with vegetables and glutinous rice for dessert. Everyone was happy, and we had a little time for ourselves. A meeting was always planned for the afternoon, and the day finished with a dance show by young Khmer Rouge soldiers, similar to those of the Chinese Cultural Revolution. The dancers were dressed in black, and mimed working methods and solidarity between the peasants and soldiers. The audience was scarcely interested; we would have preferred to have gone to bed early, but nobody dared leave until the end. The only joy for us on these days was to eat a little more than usual.

In the Kampong Cham region, the Khmer Rouge celebrated three festivals: 17 January, the date of creation of the revolutionary army in 1968; 17 April, the date of the glorious victory of the Khmer Rouge, falling on almost the same day as the Khmer New Year; and 29 September, the anniversary of the foundation of the Communist Party of Kampuchea (CPK) in 1960. These three days were the only days of rest we had per year. Despite the suppression of all religious festivals, the Old people who still lived in the villages celebrated the most important festivals secretly in their homes. They celebrated in a symbolic manner with the few means they had, and marked the *Pchum-ben* (respects paid to the dead), the *Vi-sak-bo-chea*, and the *Meak-bo-chea* (festivals commemorating the birth, Enlightenment, and death of the Buddha). They also celebrated the Khmer New Year, but these festivals were no longer occasions for spectacular productions, illuminations, fireworks, or collective games as they had once been. All the popular folklore had disappeared, and the street theatres that we were used to seeing on the stone bas-reliefs in the richly-decorated Bayon temple at Angkor, with its acrobats, jugglers, cockfights, and buffalo fights, had been crossed off the calendar. Popular joy disappeared, giving way to a sadness that could be seen on every face.

The official language, Khmer, whose alphabet is among the richest of all world languages, was retained by default by Democratic Kampuchea because it wasn't designated by the Constitution of 5 January 1976 as the national language. This omission was probably deliberate on the part of the Khmer Rouge, whose objective was to destroy the cultural importance of the Khmer language as a legacy of our identity. Article 3 of the Constitution of Democratic Kampuchea, states that the culture must be national, popular, and progressive. Our language, therefore, had to be adapted to the "new culture". The Khmer literary language was incomprehensible to the Old people who became cadres of the Angkar. The created a new way of writing that was less complex, and a new spoken language that was more rustic. The changes affected the vocabulary, its sense, and phrasing. The old language was extremely hierarchical, reflecting social life, so that the terms "I eat" or "I sleep" took on several different expressions depending on the rank of the person being spoken to, i.e. farmer or civil servant, bonze or prince, and according to one's state of mind. The term "to eat" could, therefore, be translated in several ways: *si*, a trivial expression; *nham*, a term used by city-dwellers; *pisa*, a more official term especially with regard to elderly people; *chhan*, reserved for bonzes; *saoy*, for members of the royal family. All of these terms disappeared from the language and were replaced by a single word, *hop*, meaning "to gobble". It has to be said, however, that the poor quality of our food didn't justify a nobler word than that.

Even the family and parenthood were abolished, and all representation of the genealogical structure—which is standard in family and social language—was removed from our language, according to the principle of complete equality among citizens. All words that described family networks, or that measured levels of fraternity and social solidarity, fell into disuse. In addition, we New people were obliged to watch our use of language in order to avoid being recognised as city-dwellers or "traitors of the revolution."

We had all become *pror-chea-kak-sekor*, or *kam-ma-kor*, which meant "peasant people" or "workers", and the *ka-ma-phi-bal* were the Khmer Rouge cadres[1]. In daily life, we called each other *mitt* (comrade) followed by our first names. When referring to the leaders, we used the term *mitt* followed by a term of respect, *borng*, which meant either "brother" or "sister", or *neary*, meaning "woman". New hierarchical uses of these terms appeared, and a combination of the two terms suggested a higher rank, for example "*mitt neary* Eng Heang", meaning "comrade sister Eng Heang", and suggesting she is a camp leader or cadre.

The rules of politeness which we had known from birth were also completely banished. Now, when we met someone, we no longer greeted each other with the *sam-*

[1]   According to the first article of its Constitution, Democratic Kampuchea was a state of workers and peasants.

peas, joined hands, that most gracious Khmer greeting. We no longer heard the terms *som-toaus*, "excuse me" or *or-kun*, "thank you". We no longer had any need to respect our parents or grandparents, or even elderly people in general, as we had always done. Some *dach-khat* children (children who blindly obeyed the Angkar) called their parents *mitt*: *mitt oev*, "comrade father", *mitt yeay,* "comrade grandmother". Everyone tried to disappear into anonymous verbal expressions which conformed to cadre discourse and wouldn't shock. All originality was considered a sign of resistance, and during all official or unofficial meetings, we mechanically addressed each other as *mitt*.

The new spoken language was also forged around political slogans and mottos which were quoted to us daily and taken up again during the meetings:

- "Long live the glorious 17 April, overwhelming day."
- "Long live the extremely intelligent, visionary and glorious revolutionary Angkar."
- "Down with American imperialists and their servants."
- "One hand for production, the other to combat the enemy."
- "The Angkar is a great leap forward, a phenomenally great leap."
- "When we tear out weeds, we have to tear out the roots."
- "Independence means being responsible for one's actions."

- "The Angkar is very shrewd."
- "The Angkar has pineapple eyes."
- "Sick people are victims of their imagination."
- "You must spy on the smallest actions of each and every one of you."
- "You must bend to the orders of the Angkar."
- "Keep secrets and you'll live a long life."
- "The reconstruction of oneself."
- "It is forbidden to move around freely."
- "The Angkar begs you to please…"

These phrases, both mottos and supports for the doctrine of Democratic Kampuchea, formed a basis for the cadre's language, serving them as reply and answer to practically every situation and before all daily problems. The mottos replaced speech. We discovered that the Khmer Rouge encapsulated the image of the Angkar as a new god who was omnipresent, frightening, and resourceful, and who had to be served and venerated as we had previously venerated the Buddha.

No foreign languages were spoken during the four years of the Democratic Kampuchea regime. They had become not only useless, but also dangerous, revealing a concealed level of education. Those who inadvertently used a couple of French or English words were immediately accused of being intellectuals, spies for the old regime, or even members of the KGB or the CIA, and risked their life. The cadres tried to trap us by asking us to read the symptoms on a box of medication or the instructions on a product wrapping.

Our spoken language was extremely impoverished in its number of words and phrases. It was at the linguistic level of the cadre peasants, which was very basic compared to the language we had learned at secondary school. For example, we no longer said *dek*, "to sleep", we said *sam-rak*, "to rest", emphasising the fact that sleep was just a permitted time for recovery. We no longer said *rieap-kar*, "to get married", we said *rieap-krousar* because marriage was considered a ceremony linked to the past and was replaced by a simple union. We no longer said *pkey* or *pror-pourn*, meaning "husband" and "wife", but *krousar* to designate either of the spouses indifferently. New terms appeared that were loaded with violence and Khmer Rouge ideology: *kam-tech*, "to demolish" in the sense of "to kill"; *sam-rok*, "to work like a combatant"; and *dak-kluon*, "to yield" or "to submit". It is interesting to note that now, over thirty years later, some of these terms have become part of our everyday language, such as the term *krousar* to designate both husband and wife. The meaning of the words "husband" and "wife" was deeply distorted under the regime, and the idea of a couple formed on the basis of a man and woman's mutual desire no longer existed—there were now only comrades. Some of these new expressions invented by the Khmer Rouge today shock those Khmer of the diasporas who have retained their traditional language. The rebuilding of our national identity is still mitigated through a militant defence of the Khmer language as a symbol of our cultural and social diversity.

CHAPTER 14

THE BIG WORKS PROJECTS OF DEMOCRATIC KAMPUCHEA

The Angkar employed military vocabulary to divide the camp workforce into work sites. So *kar-than stoung-srov* was the project for rice transplantation, *kar-than loeuk-tum-noptoeuk* was the dam project, and *kar-than chrot-srov* was the project for harvesting rice. My *korngchalat* was based near Phum Thmey but we were a mobile workforce and were often sent to other villages to facilitate some of the larger projects. The projects of the village of Antong Sar and Angkor Ban were among the hardest and most exhausting that we came across during the nearly four years we spent under the regime of Democratic Kampuchea.

It was November or December of 1977. The water was high, and the weather was cool, even cold. Our working day was 12 hours long, and the food rations were very small. This was the first selection process for physical resistance, and this was where we started to be screened. My friend Nany found that it was at that time, in Antong

Sar, that the work was the most exhausting and the executions more and more frequent. Comrade Run, head of the police, patrolled our worksites and the surrounding villages. We slept in huts which had only a simple roof and no partitions or walls, like those normally used to shelter animals. The Angkar had installed a row of wicker racks made from plaited young wood to serve as beds. These racks ran right along both sides of the hut, leaving a central corridor for us to get around. The *korngchalat* leaders allotted us a space of 60 cm each, and we slept side by side in our dozens. The purging inside our camp speeded up, and, every so often, girls were woken up by Khmer Rouge cadres in the middle of the night, one after another. They were taken away, and we never saw them again.

In the evenings, I heard whispered discussions between our leaders. We worked out that the *yothea* soldiers were coming to get those girls who had already lost parents or brothers. We were very afraid, and when the militia came to pick out a girl, we didn't dare get up to look. We were afraid of being accused of complacency or complicity. The next day those girls who'd been chosen were no longer there, and they never came back. Sometimes our leaders tried to hide the truth from us by announcing that the girls had been sent to join their family, or that they had been transferred to another camp, and we pretended to believe her. At other times, however, we were told officially during the evening meetings that the Angkar had decided to eliminate such and such a person, leaving the threat to hang over us.

I remember the night that the *yothea* came to get two sisters of 17 April 1975, girls I really liked. Ny and Neth were the two daughters of a primary school teacher originally from Phum Pong Ro, a village near Phum Thmey. Ny was quiet and melancholic, while her sister, who was 17 or 18 years old, was happy and as "clever as Hanuman", the king of the monkeys. I still remember her imitating people, and she often made us laugh, we who laughed so little. Neth worked in our *korngchalat*, and had adapted better than others, probably because of her optimistic personality. During meetings or at work, she asked questions and liked getting explanations, but this wasn't appreciated by the leaders who sometimes didn't know how to answer her. When her family was killed I sensed that Neth knew. We were told that her sister had been sent to join another camp, but when Neth heard this she thought her sister was in danger. She was frightened, and, without asking permission, she left to look for Ny. Everyone in our *korngchalat* guessed what would happen to the girls. We tried to look for Neth, but two hours later, the director of the security force came to speak with his colleagues, and we heard what he said: "Those two girls tried to run away, so we caught them and raped them before we stabbed them to death. We had to put them sitting, and we cut their heads off like you cut a log for the fire, but they didn't die easily. Then we wiped off the knives."

After our two friends were wiped out, I saw their executioners come back and divide up their clothes amongst themselves. The Khmer Rouge buried the bodies naked, taking their victims' black shirts and trousers. When several days had passed, we stopped talking about the two girls. We didn't dare ask questions. We had to survive. To survive . . .

Our huts rapidly became infested with vermin, crickets, scorpions, and all sorts of other insects. These huts were just temporary resting places which we passed through. We would spend a night in one hut, and the next night we'd find ourselves in another shelter of the same style. We were deprived of all personal space, something which even prison detainees are normally allowed. Nowhere could we feel safe or that we were in our own space, and this was just another way of abolishing the idea of the person. There were no individuals any more, just a mobile work force. But what did it matter, since we spent more time on the works projects than we did in the huts?

To wash ourselves, we had to walk almost a kilometre. Girls washed themselves in a pond or *boeung* reserved for women, while another pond was reserved for the men, who slept in huts a few hundred metres from ours. These ponds were the same ones used by the cooks, and they often came to fill their pots and jars with this water for cooking. During the rainy season, we simply washed in the paddy fields near our hut because, after 12 hours of work, we no longer had the strength to walk the kilometre to the pond. Some girls no longer bothered at all about personal hygiene because it reduced their time for resting.

When they arrived in the huts, they just collapsed on the wicker racks and fell asleep.

A few months later, our *korngchalat* moved to the commune of Reay Pay, in the Korng Meas district. We stayed there on two occasions, once in 1977 and again in 1978. This works project was isolated in the forest, and far from everything. The pond here was filled with cold black water which made us shiver. There was no village, no peasants, and no fruit trees, all of which would have suggested people had lived there at some point. In fact, it was nothing more than a depression that flooded during the rainy season, and in the old days the peasants didn't work this land. It was entirely undeveloped and had been reserved for the wild animals and the *neak-ta*, or earth spirits. The *neak-ta* watch over the people and are attached to particular places. They must be paid proper respect, and the idea of desecrating this virgin soil under the authority of the Khmer Rouge was a source of bad luck for us.

The weeds were long, and we were immersed in cold water to our knees or sometimes even to our chests. Each of us was given a sickle with a lengthened handle for working under water. We arrived at dawn on the first day and were immediately terrorised. We tried to stay on the dykes because we were afraid to go in the water; it was filled with snakes, leeches, and crocodiles but the Khmer Rouge sent us in anyway. We tucked our trousers in tightly, and one of the cadres set an example by going in first. It was early morning and the water was freezing. The biggest girls like me had to go in first, into the deepest places.

The earth was muddy and slippery under my feet, and I prayed hard, thinking of my parents and all our spirits so they would protect me and keep me alive. We began work at dawn, and the day only ended when darkness fell. We returned to the huts scared stiff, and were convinced we had awoken the anger of the *neak-ta*.

Around 2 a.m. the next morning, we were woken abruptly by a gong and called to "weeding combat", in the pond at Reay Pay. From about 7 or 8 a.m. we had to water the paddy fields, and this lasted until about 5 p.m. when were sent to pull and transplant rice plants. We took our evening meal of red maize around 10 p.m. The meal was accompanied by fish or meat soup, but it was so much like ditch water that we swallowed it with difficulty, even though we were ravenous. Even then, our day wasn't over because we had to chase away the rats that came to eat in the paddy fields until about midnight. During the night, we were woken once more and sent back to work. Some days we worked almost 20 hours a day and lived on red maize. Each of us asked the same question: why did our cadres send us to work in the deep water in the early morning when it was freezing, and make us do dry work when the hot sun was up? There was no rational explanation, unless their aim was to increase the severity of the work, thereby eliminating the weakest girls from amongst us. We didn't have the energy to discuss it, so we kept quiet.

The pond, after being cleared and weeded, remained unworkable. We were exhausted and frustrated by the absurdity of the forced labour. We were now painfully thin. Many girls had again stopped menstruating and several became ill. Every morning, some girls would take the risk of asking for a rest. The leader would examine them closely, and if she declared that they were not ill, they were severely punished. Corporal punishment, or death, or somewhere between the two—there was so little difference.

In 1978, the Angkar launched a project to build a storage basin in Anlong Chrey, in the Batheay district. This was a regional project, and it was the first time our *korngchalat* took part in one of these bigger projects. All the mobile workforces in the region were requisitioned to complete the task. Huts were put up in several areas near a clearing at the edge of the village, and the men's quarters were located quite far from the women's quarters. There were now fewer of us in the *korngchalat* because we had endured several purges and various successive departures. Our numbers were reduced from about 120 down to 80, and one hut was now enough to lodge our group.

On the evening of our first day in Anlong Chrey, the leaders from all levels were called together to receive instructions from the Angkar *loeu*. After the evening meal, we too were called to the meeting. The orders were very strict: each of us had to dig and carry 3 m³ of earth every day. We would be woken by the gong each day and had to proceed immediately to the work sites, without exception. Each cooperative was partitioned, and relations between men and women were strictly forbidden, as was all contact between the various *korngchalat*. Ours was a prison universe, and our country had been turned into an open air prison.

After the supervisory meeting, we went back to the huts, but our sleep was again cut short that night. We judged the time by the position of the stars and moon and could work out an approximation of the time. I guessed it was about 4 a.m. when the gong rang the next morning. We were called to work in the fields, and each of us brought two sorts of things: our bundle of possessions, which contained a can of drinking water, a plate, and a spoon, and either a pick, two baskets, or a flail. This bundle, according to the Angkar, was "the adequate property of a new people". The workers lined up in single file according to their *korngchalat* and proceeded to the worksite in silence. It was pitch black and the work sites were over two kilometres away. Each time we stopped, some of the girls stumbled, half asleep. Some pretended to go to the toilet so they could try and sleep for a few minutes.

The sharing out of jobs was upset by the Angkar's constant need to keep men and women separate. So the leaders designated another job to us; we had to dig and fill in 3 m³ of earth each. As the sun rose, I could see several hundred men and women working on the land, like ants. Revolutionary music was broadcast from the site headquarters to stimulate our work pace, and, from time to time, the *mitt-borng*, members of the superior Organisation, came and went among us to supervise our progress. They set up competitions between the various *korngchalat* to try and drive us further, and during one evening meeting the leaders announced that members of a model *korngchalat* had reached their target of 3 m³ before the end of the day. Therefore, they were increasing our daily target by another 1m³ each. Each leader would be proud if his/her team was nominated as a "strong and advanced section". Under a scorching sun, we human termites worked away to fill the enormous termite mound.

The work became harder and harder as the days passed, and the pace became faster and faster. According to the decentralised administration of Democratic Kampuchea, the mission of every *korngchalat* was to produce enough to support their own communes and districts. At midday we ate on site and, by chance, the food was improved a little during this period because of the contributions of all the regional collectives. Sometimes we got simple ordinary rice, and sometimes we got rice mixed with maize, bananas, or potatoes. When it rained, we worked with difficulty, but our leaders repeatedly told us we weren't grains of salt that would melt and, therefore, nothing should stop us making progress.

To celebrate Khmer New Year, the collective kitchen rice noodles to us, with a pinch of salt, instead of the usual fish soup. As usual, we had to thank the Angkar for this generous offering, and Vanny and I were at the end of our tethers.

After several weeks, the dam began to take shape and was finally completed after ten weeks of intensive work. It was 40 m wide and 11 m high, extending as far as the eye could see. We could hardly believe our eyes: we, with our arms and willow baskets, were really that strong! We were proud of our work because of the dam's sheer size, even if it would be of no use, as some were already saying.

It was now 1978, a year of high water, as the Khmer put it. Rumours went around that the higher cadres of the Khmer Rouge weren't getting on well amongst themselves, and that serious reshuffles were occurring in the higher echelons of the Angkar. It was said that the person in charge of the zone next to us, So Phim, had planned a coup against Pol Pot and was now dead. We heard that cadres from the western zone had come to replace the defective cadres in the eastern and central zones, where we were located. On several occasions, we saw upper cadres who had been under So Phim's authority, being transported in military trucks with their hands tied behind their backs. Some were called out during meetings and never came back. Ke Pauk, with the support of Ta Mok, took the central zone to which we belonged[1] in hand, and for more than a month we lived through a nightmare. The number of killings increased dramatically, and the spectacle of human bodies floating on the nearby Mekong gave us the shivers. Sometimes we could make out a man or a woman dressed in black with a *krama* knotted around their necks, and their hands tied behind their backs. The Mekong water became a tragic scene. It was no longer a place of

---

1   This takeover of control was sharply felt by the civil population in the central zone during 1978. See Salomon Kane, *Dictionnaire des Khmer rouges*, p. 411 f. See also Khamboly Dy, *A history of Democratic Kampuchea 1975-1979*, Documentation Center of Cambodia, 2007, p. 24.

relaxation as it had once been. During our communal baths in the river, we washed as quickly as we could, and never lifted our eyes from the surface of the water. We didn't properly understand what conflict had been settled by these mass executions. We did notice, however, that the victims floating on the water were Angkar cadres, because people like us didn't dress like that. We thought that if they were capable of killing their combat comrades, they would surely have no scruples in killing us, the inferior people. We wondered constantly, "What will happen to us tomorrow?"

The words of my Uncle Phorng, who had been a colonel in the air force and was also executed, came back to me all the time: "You have to understand," he would say, "the Khmer Rouge don't kill with a rifle, they prefer to cut your throat with the stalk of a Palmyrah, firstly because a bullet is costly for the Angkar, and, secondly, because a bullet kills faster than a Palmyrah stalk, which tends to strangle you gradually."

Nany, her sister Nyny, and I, trusted each other and wondered how we could put an end to it all. We were all Buddhists, so it wasn't easy to talk about suicide—committing suicide is a sin in our religion. I contemplated the Mekong, thinking that it might be the only place that could receive my body and soul. We knew well that sooner or later the Angkar would find some pretext to kill us, and before they killed us, what else would they do to us? We knew that the militia raped women before killing them, and that a woman interned in the O Trakuon prison had been raped collectively by members of the *San-tek-sok*[2]. They had left her to die but she managed to take refuge in a *stupa*. She stayed there for several weeks, hidden under the roof of the *stupa* until the Vietnamese troops finally arrived. She was perhaps the only survivor of the prison at O Trakuon.

The new cadres from the southwest zone were quickly distributed throughout all levels. These new arrivals spoke Khmer with a strong accent. We called them the people of the southwest, but in fact they were from Kampot and Takeo. The purging of cadres in the region continued under our very eyes. We met them several times, hands tied behind their backs, surrounded by the militia. They were on their way to be executed and didn't even try to resist. What would have been the point? Every day was a nightmare after this radical change. The regional *korngchalat* director was replaced, and our *korngchalat* leader seemed even more frightened than we were. The relatives of the *korngchalat* members experienced the same fears as we did, and to avoid punishment and death, we were all obliged to work like convicts and be constantly on the look-out.

At the end of 1978, we were sent back to Phum Thmey during the harvest period. We received an order from the highest quarters to dig a big ditch in the village. We later learned that each village had received a similar order, but at the time we had no idea what the ditch was for.

2   security force.

But our anxiety grew. According to rumours, the Angkar was going to eliminate all the New people and any Old people it considered badly reconstructed. This operation corresponded to the last stage of the purging project which the Angkar planned for early 1979. Without a doubt, we were all going to be killed, and our bodies thrown into this mass grave. We lost all hope, and I started staring at the Mekong as a place to drown myself and end the ordeal[3].

When we had built the ditch, we were moved to another works project, and we didn't know whether this would be the ultimate one. But the work turned out to be less hard than we were expecting, and we were given more acceptable food for the effort we were making. The executions also stopped. Five or six Cham girls were called out of our group, but the next day they were freed again, and we found them on the dam. We didn't understand what was going on. We began to wonder if the Angkar had somehow changed its policy…

---

3   After the fall of the regime of Democratic Kampuchea, we discovered that each *sahakor* cooperative had a ditch to hold the victims of purges. The Angkar planned to keep very few people to rebuild a new Kampuchea, the population having been reduced to people who were pure in the revolutionary sense.

CHAPTER 15

THE DESTRUCTION OF HUMAN DIGNITY

For three years, eight months, and twenty days we lived under the omnipresent eye of the Angkar, this supreme authority of barbarity. Democratic Kampuchea was a regime of deception and famine of which I have retained a complete and burning memory. The Khmer Rouge broke the family unit. But beyond the family, there was no longer any social solidarity, neither relatives nor neighbours at the heart of which an individual could identify himself, or form a network of confidence. The regime introduced distrust even in the home. Children had to devote their life to the Angkar and no longer respected their parents; their consciences were violated in front of their helpless parents. The Khmer Rouge transformed each human being into a machine devoid of all critical sense. Moved by famine and the fear of being killed, people lost all sense of each other and were capable of denouncing father, brother, or sister. This was what we had become. It was every man for himself.

The regime taught me not to trust even my closest relatives, such as my own aunt and uncle, and this forced me into solitude. Silence was a guarantee of safety, according to the expression *dam-doeum-kor*, which means "plant the kapok tree", a silent tree whose canopy stifles noise. Even feelings of friendship became suspect because they could reveal a relationship, and it could seriously compromise an Old person if he or she were to become attached to one of the New people. Some members of this unfortunate people hid their identity by simulating madness and wearing rags, their clothes were worn and dirtier than floor cloths, their hair never saw a comb, and their fetid bodies were covered in wounds and stains.

In this situation of continuous abuse, we lost all moral sense. Our behaviour, to put it mildly, could be summed up in one abiding need: to fill our stomachs. I saw all sorts of petty theft and stealing, such as the theft of food in the *korngchalat* when everyone was on the works site. Often a person who had been declared sick and granted a day of rest, took advantage of the situation to go through the bundles of his or her colleagues, looking for food. We were so hungry that the word *khlean*, meaning "to be very hungry", still resounds in my ears. On the worksite, if we were harvesting maize we stole maize, if we were harvesting rice we stole rice, or beans, or whatever else we had access to. We hid the foodstuffs inside our shirts or trousers, and the leaders knew about it, but they too were hungry and would sometimes pretend not to see. At times we even shared what we had stolen from the fields with the leaders.

Beyond such distrust inherited from the past, there is also a dull pain which remains. After all, the Khmer Rouge who had emerged from the Old people still live in their villages, unrepentant. The past hasn't been entirely swallowed up by the present. Their guilt will not be erased —could they do evil in their present or future lives? And how can we get them to repent? We will never forget that our human dignity was removed from us, that we worked like slaves and were fed like dogs.

In those days, if we had been able to read the introduction to the Constitution of Kampuchea: "To build a society where happiness, equality, justice and true democracy reign, without rich or poor, without classes that exploit or are exploited, a society in which the whole nation lives in harmony and great national unity to participate in the work of production, to build and defend the country together," we would have had an idea of the abysmal error into which Pol Pot had hastened us. We would have understood what Albert Camus denounced in 1946: "We don't think badly because we are murderers. We are murderers because we think badly. That is how one can be a murderer without ever seeming to have killed."

PART III

1979

EMERGING FROM THE NIGHT

CHAPTER 16

THE JOY OF SEEING MY FAMILY AND BEING FREE AGAIN

The nobleman protects the destitute as clothing covers a body,
The saint protects the illiterate as the sampan protects the pirogue.
The venerable Chuon Nat

On 7 January 1979, the Vietnamese took Phnom Penh, and the Khmer Rouge suddenly became invisible. We were free, and left to ourselves as I described at the beginning of this book. In the space of a single night, all the *korngchalat* were emptied of their supervisors, and we went into the villages to listen and try to work out what was happening. The Old members of the various work camps returned to their families in the village, while the New survivors left the village to go back to their own towns.

My first thought was for my family; had they survived, how could I make my way to them? I had no news of them for four years, and Siem Reap was more than 400 kilometres away. I didn't have the means or energy to make that trip on my own, and I was afraid what would happen to me if I tried to make that trip.

Instead, I went to Phum Thmey, to Ta Chourp and Yeay Pheap, my adopted family. We didn't dare broach the subject directly, instead we exchanged simple words, simple everyday words, and on hearing them, we knew something had changed. In a few hours, the village seemed to breathe easier, and began to fulfil its proper function as a place of life and meeting.

The villagers united around the director of the cooperative—who was from the same village—and they shared out the produce of the cooperative: rice, beans, maize, tobacco, tools, and so on. Those whose houses had been taken apart to build the collective buildings began to identify each beam and plank in order to reclaim them and rebuild their houses. Those who had willingly or unwillingly pooled their goods at the time of the *dak-ruom* in 1975 lost no time in reclaiming them. There were a lot of people in the cooperative, and those who dared take more simply took it; the division was a free-for-all. Ta Chourp and Yeay Pheap's family was one of those which didn't dare take too much, even though the cooperative director was Yeay Pheap's older brother. But they made sure they got back the beams and planks which they had been obliged to give up because they wanted to rebuild their house. If others couldn't find their property, they demanded indemnity from the cooperative's farming materials. Everyone then agreed to get rid of the *sahakor* because its warehouses were empty, and it no longer had any reason to exist. We were looking at a spontaneous attempt to rebuild a peasantry founded on small family farms, like those before the war.

Three or four months later, a solidarity group was formed to take charge of the current crops and the harvests. This group was absorbed into a self-help group created in each village on the initiative of the new regime, and supported by the Vietnamese. Between ten and fifteen families made up a self-help group. Families without a man were divided into different self-help groups, so they could help each other and produce more efficiently, but also to manage the population.

This was also a period of family regrouping. Everyone wanted to find their own people. The private use of dwelling houses was re-established, and would never again be questioned by the People's Republic of Kampuchea. The ownership of the land, on the other hand, remained collective. The organisation of the new regime began this time at the lowest level, before moving up to the middle level. A few weeks later, one of the villagers, Duch Krim, was designated, without too much argument, as the head of the village of Phum Thmey. He carried out a new census of the population, and redid the biography of each person as under the Pol Pot regime. I don't know who asked him to do so, but I was asked to give a hand with the writing. I had decided to join my family, however, so I declined the request.

Work in the paddy fields started again under the supervision of a leader who was chosen after discussion between the various members; this was the first step towards democracy. The crops were shared between members of the self-help groups, and the harvest would be shared out equitably, taking into account the number of participants and the size of each family. We were no longer obliged to go to the fields at 3 or 4 a.m. We still worked, but we started later, depending on the sun. At midday, if our place of work wasn't too far away, we went back to eat with our families, and then we had a little snooze, anywhere we liked—on a mat or under a mango tree. If we didn't feel well, we asked the group leader for permission to be absent. There was neither medication nor doctors, so the gurus took up their traditional treatments again. We could also eat as much as we wanted. We were able to gather fruit and vegetables around each house again, without fear, and the production of family gardens was no longer destined for the collective.

Freedom returned in simple things. Women who had managed to hide coloured clothes or jewellery in the hollow of a tree or buried in the ground, shared these with their daughters. We exchanged, with inexpressible joy, lots of everyday products: fish, freshly killed meat, vegetables, fruit and so on. In the evening, after a dinner eaten in the setting sun, we visited people on the other side of the road or village. Those who played music put together instruments as best they could, the *kong-toch* or the *kong-thom* (high or low gong chimes), the *tro*, the *sko-thom* (double drums), the *chapei* (big curved guitar), the *sko* (drum), and improvised music in twos or threes. Young boys and girls saw each other freely after work; some made *am-bok*, ground rice, under the moonlight. Each evening we heard the sounds of adults and children laughing, music and songs, and—this really impressed me—the dull sound of pestles ringing out from one house to another, announcing the family meal. The streets swelled once more with happy sounds.

Four months later, on 13 April 1979, the Khmer New Year reappeared on our calendar, to our immense joy. We prepared for it feverishly. For the first time in almost four years, we were free. Finally we could do what we wanted after work: we could wander around the village, or simply sit on a mat and listen to the voices in the street. How good it felt!

We came back to our traditional Khmer New Year games. The most well-known is *boh-angkonh*, named after an oval wild fruit that looks like a kneecap, and is a brown colour in a shiny shell. As soon as the festival was announced, children and young people got together in two camps, one for the boys and one of girls, to confront each other at *boh-angkonh*. Each side placed its pods in a line in the sand and, as in a game of skittles, you had to knock over the line of pods by throwing other *angkonh* at them. The winning side was allowed to hit each member of the opposing team on the knee—as a doctor checks the knee jerk reflex with a hammer—then take advantage of the situation to stroke the knee or ankle of the adversary. According to tradition, those who didn't respect the rule risked bad luck or worse, being struck by lightning! The risk increased the desire of the player or the temptation to lose. We also played *chaul-chhoung*. Boys and girls faced each other with a ball knotted into a *krama*, this was the *chhoung*, in a kind of prisoner ball game. The loser had to carry the winner or sing or dance. Early attempts at seduction were directed in this way through games, in a society that was prudish and puritanical, and where flirting was an offence.

The first signs of Buddhist practice also reappeared, giving us confidence. But were we worthy of any generosity? Was it possible for the course of our life to change? By the time the "mango showers" began, some men were already prepared to take their vows. The deserted pagodas would live again; they had their place in the cycle of harvests and there was no time to lose. These men were the oldest in the community, widowers, or men without family who were encouraged to go to the pagoda and honour the Buddha. With each symbol that was reinstated, life reappeared and all the old customs began to fall into place again.

Solidarity was expressed without reserve. We shared everything, even our houses. We were afraid to live in a big house with too much space, so we slept close to each other, as tradition had it, on the first floor, united in a communal room on a bamboo floor. If one's parents, brothers, or sisters were dead or had disappeared, the house was abandoned to others who would give it new life. Everywhere people settled where there were other people, and the villages were reformed around new centres, a living tree attracting others.

The idea of getting rich was absent from our minds. We still thought only of filling our stomachs each day. Everything was scarce, but we didn't care. We had the impression we were living in paradise. What a change! Freedom filled the air, it was there, it was palpable, it rang in our heads like music. Joy settled in, and our dreams became reality.

But what if the Khmer Rouge were to return? We never stopped thinking about that possibility. It was always at the back of our minds, but no one dared ask the question aloud; it was as if they might hear us. We put our fears to one side, however, and concentrated on rebuilding our lives. Young single people got together, dreaming again of having a family. Parents who had found their children wanted to marry them, after four years of being prevented from doing so. A breeze of liberty recalled our traditions, our ancient habits. We were free to build our lives again, to move around without permission of the local authorities, free to talk to each other, to meet each other, and to get married. But the return to our daily life was in no way ensured: there was nothing to buy or sell, everything was scarce, and yet the establishing of a family unit again seemed like a priority far greater than all our other needs, such as rebuilding houses, or looking for a trade or a job.

We thought of nothing but marriage, the word appeared in all our conversations and projects. Parents of boys spent their time looking for future daughters-in-law, while the parents of girls enquired about the behaviour of future sons-in-law. I noticed that the young people took advantage of a freedom they hadn't had before 1975, and boys and girls met each other secretly to get to know each other better. They were now able to meet and had the right to see each other before the wedding. Certain principles had given way. But who would have stopped them, since they were often orphans? The Khmer Rouge tragedy, combined with the deprival of marriage for almost four years, had made parents more tolerant. For the moment, the old customs didn't have the same restrictive character. Marriage was the main preoccupation among the thousand hardships we were trying to forget. Wedding music could be heard every day, and everyone was busy with wedding feast preparations. In the country, when there was a wedding, all the villagers extinguished their kitchen fires and went to the wedding. This tradition was followed in almost all villages.

For the moment, we were short of everything, but to prepare a wedding, numerous preliminaries had to be respected. Even if we were still living in difficult conditions, the concern to recover our dignity by renewing our ancient traditions inspired us all. For a start, the boy's family would ask a member of their family, or a close relative of the girl, to go to her house and get things started. If the boy no longer had any parents, he could ask a close relative to take on the role. On the day of the engagement, the boy's family brought presents of fruit, cakes, and sometimes jewellery to give to the family of the future bride. If the parents of the girl agreed, the two families then got together again to fix a date for the wedding, and to share the cost of the ceremony between the two families. At that time, I often heard the parents of a boy propose gifts such as a cow, a pig, a sack of rice, and some clothes for the future bride's family. The gifts were offered in proportion to the modest heritage of each family.

The traditional marriage festival is always celebrated in the family of the bride, and I still remember the simplicity of these marriages. The parents from both sides invited people from their families and their friends, and the guests were given the job of helping with various tasks: building huts for the celebration, cooking, preparing the traditional ceremony, carrying water, killing animals, preparing the meat, and so on. A woman was designated to look after the married couple as well as the bridesmaids and groomsmen. Great excitement accompanied all these preparations, which were for us moments of freedom and new-found joy.

In order to build the huts where the wedding guests would be lodged, bamboo trunks or logs had to be found, plus curtains, canvas, and tarpaulins. At that time Khmer money—the riel—hadn't reappeared, so barter was again the thing. Everything was pooled. If we were lacking anything, we exchanged rice, jewellery recovered from a hollow tree trunk, tobacco, maize, green beans, or anything which had trading value. People also helped each other out: today it was your turn, and tomorrow you would come to my house. Women helped do the cooking, while men helped the *achar*, a ritual specialist, to prepare the numerous things necessary for the traditional ceremony. This included getting the offerings ready, ordering the music to be played during the ceremony, organising the ringing of the gong, preparing the gifts, etc. The groomsmen and bridesmaids were also designated to help out. Nobody escaped this system of exchange and solidarity which was slowly recreating the social network that had been cut off during the black years.

I was involved in the preparations for multiple weddings. The villagers asked me to be stylist, hairdresser, and make-up expert. They also counted on my city training and education—that I had hidden for so long—to help and guide them. They asked for my opinion on how the couple should dress, because city-dwellers, and people from Siem Reap, are known for having stronger traditions than the inhabitants of the banks of the Mekong. I tried to make the bride and groom beautiful. At this time, in 1979 and 1980, we didn't have much. I had hidden a silk *sampot* and a little lace blouse, which I lent to several brides. Some girls had also managed to secrete a few cosmetics, such as a powder compact, an eye pencil, lipstick, and *eau de toilette*. All the brides wanted my services, and I was very happy to do them a favour in conditions that weren't easy. But we had become used to such hardship and were well able to improvise.

I will mention just two friends' weddings in which I actively participated; this was the marriage of Phann, Ta Chourp and Yeay Pheap's daughter, and also Vanny's marriage. Phann was marrying Reth, the son of a family of Old people from the same village, while Vanny was marrying You Sakhaunn. Both Vanny and You Sakhaunn were New people of 1973. I noticed that the Old people continued to marry Old people, and the New people married amongst themselves. The difference of status still encountered a certain reticence and the tension between the two groups, fanned by Democratic Kampuchea, hadn't gone away. The social network was still fragile and it was easier to trust those who had shared the same status under the Angkar.

Before the wedding took place, the parents of the groom brought two sacks of rice weighing 100 kg, a pig, and a cow to feed the guests. We were still afraid of the return of the Khmer Rouge and the Pol Pot regime, and we weren't sure how far we could go with our new liberty. We were careful about everything. Ta Chourp, still submitting to the Angkar rule, went to ask permission of the head of the village to celebrate the marriage of his daughter. The ceremony began at dawn with the *sompé-lea*, to ensure that the weather would be favourable for the celebration of the marriage. Next there came the procession of gifts from the family of the groom to the family of the bride, followed by a blessing of the young couple by the rare bonzes. The union was then celebrated after a prayer to the ancestors who blessed the new couple. Tradition then required that the families attach a red thread to the wrists of the happy couple, while wishing them eternal union, happiness, longevity, and prosperity. The ceremony finished with a wedding feast for members of both the families and their guests. After the feast, the couple and their guests danced the *ram-vong*. The boys of the village entertained the wedding party with traditional and popular musical instruments, such as the *ram-vong*, the *ram-kbach* and the *lam-liev*. Those instruments, which had been possible to hide from the Khmer Rouge, brought our traditions back to life after the black years.

But in spite of this new freedom, the presence of the Khmer Rouge remained close to us and floated on the air. To hold a ceremony at our houses, whether a marriage or a Buddhist ceremony, we still had to ask the authorisation of the head of the village. In some villages, these were the same heads as during the Khmer Rouge regime. The registration of a marriage in the commune didn't exist yet, but the country people completely ignored the rules. As in the old times, they thought they were married because they held a traditional ceremony at home, and that was it. There has always been confusion between civil and traditional marriage in our culture.

These new couple hadn't been trained in the difficulties of life. They had grown up during the Khmer Rouge period and hadn't yet learned to live. Their only experience of life was under the Pol Pot regime, and they hadn't experienced a life of freedom. Now they were married, but they continued to live in the house of the bride's parents. The Chinese and Vietnamese tell us that it is "a tradition to marry a husband" because, after the marriage, the husband comes to live at the wife's house. With the Khmer it is "tradition to marry the wife", because after the marriage the wife has to move into her husband's house.

Many children were born during this period, but the young parents encountered many difficulties. They had no means of knowing how to cope with things that hadn't existed in their village under the regime, and when their children grew up, they did exactly the same thing as their parents. They got married at 25 for the boys and 18 for the girls, and life went on. Little by little, from one generation to another, the peasants restored the same rituals.

In the village where I was living, the single people of marrying age were all children of Old people—almost 80 girls, and about 60 boys. Most of these were married during the first three months after the liberation of 7 January 1979. Some of the girls waited a few months longer, but they weren't long in marrying too. The marriage, by spontaneous will of the villagers, took on a role in the re-socialisation of the nation, acting as a symbol of our recovered humanity.

PART III

1979

EMERGING FROM THE NIGHT

CHAPTER 17

RETURN TO THE VILLAGE

Your name indicates your origins. Your attitude indicates your family.

Khmer proverb

After our liberation by the Vietnamese in 1979, and having had no news of my own family since before the Khmer Rouge regime, I remained for almost four months more with Ta Chourp and Yeay Pheap. I was able to send two letters to my family thanks to people who were going to Siem Reap to trade their produce for imported merchandise from Thailand. Imagine my joy when I learned that one of my letters had reached my mother. She replied saying she had survived, as had my brother and sisters, at the other end of the country. My decision was made: I had to go and join them.

I said goodbye to the families who had supported me during that most difficult period, particularly the family of Ta Chourp and Yeay Pheap: I thanked them for having fed me, and for having hidden my background among them, without which I would surely be dead.

A few days later, some of the villagers of Phum Thmey were going to Siem Reap to do some more trading, and this was my chance to join my family. The family of Ta Chourp and Yeay Pheap gave me my share from the self-help group which had been created in every country village after the retreat of the Khmer Rouge, because I had worked with them during those four months. They gave me a little sack of tobacco which was lighter than rice, so I could exchange it for food during my journey. I left the family with tears in my eyes. The villagers let me put my bundle in their cart so I could walk unhampered. We walked across the provinces of Kampong Cham, Kampong Thom, and Siem Reap, a journey of 250 km. After several days' walk, my Ho Chi Minh sandals—made from scooter wheels—were worn out, and I had blisters all over both feet. The villagers I was travelling with were very united and kind. They invited me from time to time to sit in their cart, and at night I slept in a hammock beside them. We still feared the Khmer Rouge and knew they weren't far away and often passed by on the way to their villages. We stopped regularly to rest, to let the oxen rest, and to look for fodder. The journey on foot was very long indeed, and over ten days later we finally arrived in Siem Reap.

I went to what had been our house in the hopes of finding my family members who had survived, but I found the house occupied by Vietnamese troops instead. The commandant on duty told me the house had been

empty when he came across it. I was very worried. The
next morning in the market, I met a man who lived in
Kralanh, a district some 54 km from the centre of Siem
Reap. He was called Mr Sun and knew my family. Mr
Sun confirmed that my mother was alive, but he had no
idea what had happened to my grandmother or to my
brother, my sisters, and my cousins. The following day I
left the merchants who had accompanied me from Phum
Thmey and, together with Mr Sun, I headed feverishly
for Kralanh by bike. My intense impatience had given
me wings. I arrived at the house in Kralanh in the late
afternoon, just as my mother was getting ready to go
looking for me. She was planning to take advantage of
a Vietnamese army truck that was travelling towards
Kampong Cham. It was another piece of sheer luck that
I reappeared just at the right time. My four sisters, my
brother, and my three cousins—who had been living in
my mother's care since the death of their own parents—
had all survived. This reunion was a moment of extreme
emotion for all of us. There we were, in the family house
which my mother had managed to keep, despite the fears
of my younger brother who preferred a small cell[1] where
he said he felt much safer. Of all our family that had been
living in Phnom Penh, I was the only one they ever saw
again. All our uncles, aunts, and cousins living in Phnom
Penh had died of hunger or had been executed, including
my brother Kolbotr.

---

1   *Kum-rou* houses, see Glossary.

We were short of everything, but hope had returned. Following upon small rural commerce, regional commerce reappeared. People from Kampong Cham and Kampong Thom brought their harvest—things like tobacco, sesame seeds, and beans—which they exchanged for merchandise imported from Thailand by the border population. This merchandise included commodities like drugs, fabrics, sarongs, towels, blankets, plastic mats, white sugar, condensed milk, utensils, soap, detergent, and even small cosmetics. In a very short time, barter became widespread once more, and facilitated the return of commerce between the regions. Gold remained an exchange commodity, but it had also become a form of money, like an instrument of exchange. We bought everything with gold. We even used gold to buy small plastic utensils, make-up, clothes, or to pay for a meal. Rice served as a standard of measure of the value of food, and as a means of exchange for smaller purchases. Gold that had been hidden away reappeared in the hands of Old people, or Khmer Rouge managers who had become anonymous again. These people had accumulated the securities and jewellery of city-dwellers during the deportations of 1975. The Old people gave up these securities for the benefit of the travelling merchants—who were quickly making a fortune, and becoming the newly-rich city-dwellers. The gold that New people had exchanged with peasants for food in 1975, now went to these new merchants. Gold travelled and the various social groups were reconstituted.

The Old people had major needs in order to reconstitute their agricultural property and equip their houses. I noticed that many of them didn't know how to organise themselves to rebuild the lives they had known before 1975. Small travelling jewellery merchants hurried to install their little scales, and to provide a service for weighing and buying jewellery. Many of them took advantage of the ignorance of the Old people, especially to get hold of their gold or precious stones. Business took off again shakily, with its professionals and its petty larceny.

The people from several provinces went to Siem Reap or Sisophon and even to Poipet to buy goods. The Thais living in the border areas took the risk of crossing the border to do business with us Khmer, who were hungry for everything. Because the Khmer like to tell a joke, they told those Thais who didn't know Cambodia that there were little hills of gold all over the country, where we could collect as many little pieces of gold as we wanted.

Everyone needed supplies, everything from cutting tools that would also serve as weapons, to hammocks for sleeping in. People went as far as Poipet, the district bordering Thailand, and business traffic reappeared on the roads. The population living near Vietnam also bought Vietnamese produce, but Thai produce was better liked than Vietnamese because the Thais hadn't suffered from the war economy which had been making an impression on Vietnam for over twenty years. The foreigners stayed in little groups of between three and ten people for security reasons. The Khmer Rouge were still hiding here and there, and in the places they had vacated, they were often replaced by thieves.

More than a year after the liberation of 7 January 1979, Ta Chourp and Yeay Pheap, who had looked after me like I was their daughter, made the journey to visit me in Kralanh. This was an opportunity for my mother to thank them for having given me the support and warmth of a home when I was so much in need of it. The reassembling of families, and the search for those who had disappeared, was our main preoccupation in the beginning. With a semblance of freedom, daily life began to take on the appearance it had once had. Schools and markets reopened, often in precarious conditions, but nobody complained. We lived from day to day, and took each day as it came. Numerous houses were empty and everyone settled where they could.

Moving around was difficult but possible, and rice was still serving as a bargaining chip in 1980. It was in that year that I made my first journey to Battambang to try and find my friends from the Preah Monivong high school. A classmate had told me that there were very few survivors from the school, and some had already left the area to join refugee camps in the Thai border areas, with a view to going somewhere else. Fear remained rife, and we saw new waves of departure. Many people tried to get across the border into Thailand again, as they had tried to do in 1975. Tens of thousands of people took the road to the refugee camps all along the Thai border. Many were pushed forcibly by the Thai authorities into zones where mines had been laid in the Dangrek mountain chain, and then abandoned. A large proportion of my mother's family wanted to leave the country, with a view to emigrating towards Canada or the United States. Twenty years of war and uncertainty resulting from the presence of the Vietnamese army, had led many people to take to the roads in exile. People sought out their relatives in France, the United States, Canada, or Australia. Those who didn't have any family elsewhere also wanted to leave, but didn't know where to go. Some sought out the protection of soldiers in the new Cambodian army—or even the Khmer Rouge—to get across the border. Others set off on the route to the west without maps or help. In both cases, the risks were great and the results aleatory. My mother too was tempted to leave, but we had no close family abroad, and there were too many of us. She sent me to check out the refugee camps on the border. I went there with several villagers, and found a few friends and teachers from the secondary school in Battambang. But the situation in the camps didn't inspire confidence in me, and I returned to my mother discouraged. Later, she tried to send my brother abroad by means of a smuggler, who asked for an exorbitant fee. She had to give up, however, and we decided to stay where we were.

From travellers, I learned that Phnom Penh had been liberated. The capital was a gigantic cinema set with nobody in it. When the population heard the news on the radio on 7 January 1979, broadcast by the "National Union Front" and the Vietnamese army, they poured towards the capital. Roadblocks were installed by the army at the entrances to the city in order to control the anarchic tide of arrivals, into what had been a ghost town for several years. The question now was whether the State could be recreated in a day. The Khmer rouge had systematically emptied the houses and shops of all their furniture and goods. Trucks and cars had also been regrouped. In order to live self-sufficiently, the Khmer Rouge had set up storage sites according to the type of object or material. The silverware was kept in the building of the Council of Ministers, and the clothing, scooters, engines, rice, dried fish, furniture, shoes, household appliances, etc. were stocked in compartments[2] all around the market. The stocks were allocated to the various new ministries or municipalities, but the ministries were also empty.

People got together and settled along the main roads where there was a semblance of life. Members of the National Union Front launched an appeal for former civil servants of the old regime, as well as executives of the Khmer Rouge regime, to make themselves known. But this call awoke bad memories, and only 100 former civil servants presented themselves. These were selected to organise the new administration. But three months after liberation, the city was still deserted. The few civil servants that were in the city were living in their administrative offices. They both ate and slept there. The older ones trained the younger ones. There were no means of transport or fuel, and the rare civil servants settled into the houses located near their place of work. Little by little, people turned up to be recruited, even though

2   Houses with narrow facades, referred to in Vietnam as "shoeboxes".

the allowance to public officials was modest: 16 kg of rice per month until 1981. From 1981 to 1991, they received 20 to 30 riels plus a ration in kind: rice, sugar, candles, oil, fabrics, and petrol. Electricity and water were free, and transport to one's place of work was ensured by each ministry. Real estate didn't exist. The first functionaries recruited, were fed from collective canteens because they didn't have any lodgings. I remember that the collective canteen was still functioning in 1983 when I took part in a political training course in Phnom Penh. I received bed and board in the boarding school of the party, now the Faculty of Arts. The week's work finished on Saturday evenings, and Sunday was a day of rest. Curfew was fixed at 7 p.m., but became more relaxed from 1985 on.

Each neighbourhood was attached to a particular ministry which organised life there. The administration designated accommodation for each new person arriving in the city. But the people who were in charge of this were rapidly snowed under. The work was too slow, and pressure from the population too high. Finally people were allowed to enter the city without being controlled, and they settled in wherever they could. The villas, when they were habitable, were reserved for members of the party, experts, and army officers. In 1980 the municipality of Phnom Penh called on the teaching corps to help with the census of the urban population. The result was modest, the city counted only 90,000 civilians in 1980, and most of those were the families of civil servants.

In Phnom Penh, as in the rest of the country, small barter shops were set up at the entrance to each neighbourhood. Rice served as money until 1980 and the riel wasn't put back into circulation by the "Red Bank" until 1981. We didn't move around properly until 1985 because there was no means of transport. To get out of town or change province you needed a special authorisation for security reasons. Only civil servants could move around in official groups. Whenever I was appointed to the court in Siem Reap, I sometimes had to come on assignment to Phnom Penh. I would have to wait for a convoy of trucks transporting merchandise between Phnom Penh and Siem Reap. Often the Khmer Rouge attacked trucks circulating on the roads, and it took a whole day to cover 100 km.

During those years of great poverty, the administration didn't seem to receive any outside aid, except that which transited through the Vietnamese army, because the United Nations only recognised the power of the Khmer Rouge, who had withdrawn into Thailand. It seemed that much-bruised Cambodia was being held in quarantine by the international community.

Communism first descended on Asia in the 1970s but, as far as I can see, it never generated as much violence or as much poverty as in Cambodia. I won't make any comparison with the Chinese Cultural Revolution of 1966, because the circumstances were very different. In China, it was a question of a conflict between different political factions which led to civil servants and intellectuals being moved to the provinces. But the fate of the intellectuals and city-dwellers carried along in the storm of the Red Guard, never reached the level of violence and abuse that we experienced here[3], where the progressive failure of Democratic Kampuchea generated waves of reprisals and purgings which ultimately reached a crescendo of violence. The accumulated misfortunes of our people proved that those powerless and silent people who saw in it a sign of the anger of the *neak-ta,* were right; as opposed to those who pretended to be masters of the land and water, but who had caused distress and famine. The greatest error of the Khmer Rouge was to have had the insane pretentiousness to hinder the sacred rhythm of life.

---

3   See Chow Siao-Ling, *La Vie quotidienne d'une famille chinoise pendant la révolution culturelle,* Acropole, 1984.

PART IV

BEYOND THE KHMER ROUGE

CHAPTER 18

28 YEARS LATER

*Your family is there waiting for you. Oh my dear ones, don't
wander in these places in the woods. With the sugar cane in my
hand, I shake it, and I call you loudly. Oh my dear ones, I see all
the paths far away.*

A Khmer ritual text from the Hau Pralung

My family and I, like most of the survivors, made
a new start. The reconstitution of the family
unit leaned heavily on grandparents, who
were obliged to make up for parents that had disappeared.
My grandmother took charge of the orphan cousins that
my mother had taken in, while my mother fought to raise
her six children after my return in June 1979. She had
lost her land, and we no longer had any paddy fields. We
survived from the small activities of informal trade, and
my mother took up sewing again. At the end of 1979, the
authorities who had been put in place by the Vietnamese
asked me to join the administration of the district.
Shortly afterwards, I was nominated as President of the

Women's Association. Then my brother left for Vietnam to continue his studies, and two of my sisters went back to school after a long interruption. My other two sisters weren't able to go back to secondary school because the school didn't exist yet. As for me, I joined the young magistracy of the new People's Republic of Kampuchea at the beginning of 1983. Thus my father's dream became a reality, with the encouragement of my mother who was, nonetheless, losing the support of her eldest daughter to help care for the younger ones. Today, I continue to practise my profession in the highest jurisdiction in the country.

One day, I was on assignment in the province of Kampong Cham when a friend suggested we visit Phum Thmey. I hesitated. I even felt afraid. I didn't want to see the open air prison where I had lived for almost four years, but I relented and decided to walk straight towards the object of my fear. During that first visit, I only found the site of the camp. My hope, from then on, was to see again those who had welcomed me and whom I hadn't seen for almost twenty years.

In 1996 the village wasn't safe, and the Khmer Rouge were still in the region. I was again travelling in the village, accompanied by my colleagues from the Kampong Cham law courts and escorted by the police. The villagers of Phum Thmey, seeing the white cars, took us to be a humanitarian mission and came running. There was great emotion when they recognised me, particularly Ta Chourp and Yeay Pheap. Asian people don't hug, but our hands crossed, and we modestly placed a hand on each others' shoulders.

In those days, the roads weren't passable. People were poor, but free. They lived by working the land and staying in the same place. Ta Chourp and Yeay Pheap still lived in their clean little house, which they had rebuilt after taking apart the collective buildings and recovering the planks and beams they had had to give up to the *sahakor*. Their children were all married and lived nearby, but inside their house, nothing had really changed. All the family sat on a basic bamboo floor, the same place where they ate, slept, and chatted with their nearest and dearest. The very modest accessories of the house were still in the same place.

I also kept in touch with some of the other villagers of Phum Thmey, those who had helped me survive, but hadn't been as lucky as me. I was able to exploit the educational assets I'd acquired before 1975, but they had remained in the rural world, the one which dominated the 1980s. The social and economic revival which followed the Paris Agreements and the setting up of new institutions had taken place without them. Poverty still affected them more.

Another day in 2000, I was walking along an avenue in Phnom Penh when someone called out "Borng Tha", the name I had been given in Phum Thmey. I jumped at the name, but when I turned around I saw it was my friend Vanny. So there we were: at least two survivors of the *korngchalat*. Since that encounter we have seen each other often, and Vanny was my first and most loyal supporter when I began this initiative to record the past.

When I decided to write this account, my husband, Borng Do, also encouraged me. I wanted to clarify the past and master my feelings better. But I had to come back to the places I'd lived under the Khmer Rouge regime. I had to call up my painful memories, tread on them, and collect testimonies. Each time I had to go to Phum Thmey, I hesitated. I found pretexts to postpone the visit until later. I asked myself whether this initiative was going to liberate me from the past or, on the contrary, revive my nightmares. When it comes to emotional healing, we Asians count on the passage of time and images of the present, which pile up on top of our memories, blocking them out and replacing them.

Westerners, on the other hand, make more use of talking about the past, and its therapeutic role. I had my doubts, but I hoped that these visits and encounters would help free me from the after-effects of the past. It was very difficult. I wanted to heal, because for me the past was a chronic illness which stuck to my spirit. It would sometimes go away, but then it would come back again, so I knew I had to do something other than wait for time to heal my memories. Rithy Panh, the acclaimed Cambodian film director and screenwriter, says that this nightmare is anchored in the mind of Cambodians like a nail in the head. But how to extract it? By talking and writing. To recount a journey in order to forget it—no, I don't want to, and I won't forget it—but I had tried for too long to internalise those four years which had so affected my life. Since I have started writing, and reliving those events, I have revisited the places where I lived, and the villagers receive me gladly. I help them to share their memories and the images which reappear as quickly as their nightmares.

During a visit to Phum Thmey in December 2006, one of the leaders of our *korngchalat*, Eng Heang, came to see me. She was now married with five children. Her husband was ill, and she stayed in the background in silence, clearly not flourishing and not happy. I asked her for news of people with whom we had lived for almost four years, and she told me Srean was also married with five children. Both women were living in a village near Phum Thmey. Ta Chourp, Yeay Pheap, and their children all came out to see me, and by now they all knew me. Some of their neighbours came too. All the men were wearing a simple *krama* around their hips, with their chests completely bare. Their house was still in the same place, and one of their daughters was staying with them, but nothing else had changed. There were clothes hung out everywhere, and the house was as dusty as if it had never been inhabited. Yet it was occupied by people whose hopes were in shreds, like their mosquito net. The surroundings of the house were bare and without greenery. Under the stilts, mud and animal excrement had accumulated. Yeay Pheap sent her daughter to prepare a meal, as if to excuse herself for having nothing to offer a guest.

The old leaders, who have managed to join their families after the fall of Democratic Kampuchea, now live in hiding. They don't show themselves at festivals or during the various events organised by the villagers. Since 1979, Eng Heang has only appeared rarely. Vanny, who still has family in this village, has only met her two or three times at village festivals. I guess that for her, the perpetrator, the memory of the Khmer Rouge regime is even more painful than for me, the victim.

According to rumours, Srean was also living a nightmare. I heard she was in very bad health and that she too lived in hiding, only appearing very rarely. She would go to the fields, but as soon as she had to cross the street, she'd cover her head with a *krama*. Vanny, who now lives in the city, noticed that in her own family jealousy had poisoned the relationship between those who had moved to Phnom Penh and acquired a small shop, and those who still lived in the village. The villagers refused to meet with the members of their family who had been classified as New people under the regime. They still pretended that city people were capitalists or exploiters. These antagonisms, which the Khmer Rouge had promised to extirpate, remain anchored in the mentality of the peasants.

It wasn't until September 2007 that I saw Srean in person again. And at last, 28 years after the events, she began to talk without fear. She said she had accepted the job as leader under duress and hadn't enjoyed it. From the beginning, she told me she was gripped by fear, but had had to hide her anxiety. She said she had tried everything to protect all the girls in her care, especially those of 17 April. She regretted the disappearance of Nga, whom she said hadn't listened to her advice: she had wanted to visit her family in the village and was caught by the sinister police of the security forces. As for Neth, Srean said she got scared when she learned that her sister Ny had been taken away by the Angkar police, so she went off to look for her without permission. The police guards caught and executed her in one of the buildings of the pagoda in O Trakuon.

Srean told me she had often heard talk of the prison of O Trakuon among the Khmer Rouge cadres, but that she hadn't known what went on inside. During meetings with superiors of the Angkar *loeu*, she hadn't heard the word "massacre" or "execution". However, she did add— and her evidence is rare and of major importance, "They didn't use the word 'to kill', rather I usually heard 'to send someone for retraining' or 'to move house' or 'to a change of job'." However, with time, she began to understand what it might mean. Until this day, although she lives just a few kilometres from the pagoda of O Trakuon, she has never dared go near it.

"Borng Tha," she said to me, "I recognised your background, but I did everything I could to hide it. I was forbidden to share meals with you, but I needed your support and your knowledge, and I wanted to protect you. Do you remember that I advised you to make an effort to hide your Siem Reap accent, but it wasn't easy, and from time to time it came out naturally? The police comrade Run, chief of the *San-tek-sok* when we were in Angkor Bann, threatened me, saying that we were only to keep the 'big grains of rice, and eliminate the impurities which didn't correspond to our standards'. I knew he was thinking of girls like you. Thirty years afterwards, I am living a nightmare. I still see the monstrous excavation works which I was assigned to organise at an infernal speed. How could I force you to respect the order to move 3 cubic metres of earth per day, per woman? Now I have to look after my children, but the anxiety won't go away. My husband suggested that I shouldn't listen to information about the Khmer Rouge period. My health is poor, I have attacks of *sreut*, neurological dystonia, and at night I can't sleep unless I take sleeping pills. Since the end of that period, I can no longer stand sad situations, they give me insomnia and cause tetany crises."

Srean still remembered the pink bra and the Palmyrah leaf hat that I had made for her with bits and pieces. She had held on to them carefully. For the first time, she dared to express herself sincerely, and I felt she was relieved for it. Until then, she had thought that Vanny and I didn't want to talk to her.

Twenty-eight years later, as in 1979, there was neither water nor electricity in the village, and the street is still a dirt track. None of the children had been able to get away from their humble origins through education. This was a striking observation: progress had happened elsewhere, but not here. The people still live among themselves; they didn't develop simply because they were free. That was all. None of them knew that a special court had been set up to try the Khmer Rouge leaders. When I mentioned the existence of this tribunal to the villagers, some of their faces changed and some closed up. Fear still squats in Cambodia's history. Ta Chourp and Yeay Pheap's son-in-law told me that the people in the village had done everything to protect me from the Khmer Rouge. I know that I owe them my life.

As for Nany, she had never told the secrets of that time to her husband or her children. The ghosts of the Khmer Rouge time came back to her mind often, and at night she had nightmares. She lived in the same village, Phum Rong Ro, where she is a teacher in the primary school. I noticed that she wasn't happy, and she had changed a lot. Nany was now fragile and often ill. I no longer recognised the girl I had known in the *korngchalat*, who was funny and cheerful, and taunted death. I felt that she'd been broken. She had never been able to confide in anyone, and her children never mentioned the past to her; they didn't believe in it and were busy with other things.

Kim Touch has faced the trauma better, even though her husband was executed and she had saved only one son. In 1980 she joined the administration of the new regime, set up in her village by the Vietnamese. She came back to settle in Phnom Penh in 1990. Today, she sells newspapers in the market. For her, the poverty of the countryside is still greater than that of the city. She says that her character was forged by her ordeals, and that the work we had to do, helped her to cope with the nightmare. But she won't ever forget what she suffered under the Pol Pot regime.

These women that I found again had kept an open wound that troubled their nights. Many had gotten married just after the end of the nightmare, probably moved by a long-repressed need for protection and motherhood. But the subject often remained taboo for their husbands and family. As for their children, they remained incredulous; they had better things to do than relive the story of their parents or grandparents. So the historic reality was evaded. Today's Cambodia lives through pictures and video, not through writing. For women like Srean who were in charge of us, and who had the right of life or death over us, there must be added remorse, silence about the past, and social or family isolation. Enlisted by force, they were as terrorised as we were and subject to the same risk of being wiped out. All of them need this work of talking and memory.

According to the testimonies of Nany, Vanny, and Srean, there were only four of us among the daughters of the New people who survived: Nany, Nyny, Srourn (who had links in the village), and myself. The villagers of Phum Thmey told me that I had been lucky because "*toeuk-doh-mday-thlay*", which means that my mother's milk was precious and had protected me. The other girls had disappeared over the months without a trace, as if they had gone out to meet death. It is in their memory that I have written this book. When I mention their names in this text, their faces come back to me as if frozen, one after another, as in the nautical parades of the Water Festival. As for the 1973 girls like Vanny, they were relatively spared. Thus the purging was carried out very methodically to the end. My survival was only an exception.

It is now up to us to defend our rights as women in Khmer society, a society which progresses in tiny steps like the *apsara* dancers. The poverty of the 1980s provoked the mobilisation of women to improve their lot. In Cambodia, there is a majority of women. In towns, many women have jobs because of the low salaries their husbands earn. They dominate the shop keeping sector, and spill over broadly into the informal domain. Young girls attend school, first primary school, then fewer attend secondary school, and still fewer attend third level, in spite of their high rates of success there. The ancestral model of woman as the person in charge of the house and the housekeeping is beginning to change. This situation, in which the man looks at the world, and the woman looks at the man, is slowly changing. In Asia, progress works more by imitation or contagion than by decree. The principle of non-discrimination is certainly recognised in the Constitution of 1993, but the Constitution is seen more as a tribute than anything else.

Little by little, a desire has arisen in women's minds: that of escaping a domestic life which can sometimes be deprecating and humiliating. It was also useful to see some sociological aspects in motion: the rise in the number of divorces at the woman's initiative, new ways of life, and the strong presence of women in the world of work and in civil society.

Today, women who have responsibilities outside their household are not always acceptable to men, or even to other women. This is where we must begin. It is a question of identity and of image, but how to change this attitude? The Moslem women of Cambodia are experiencing still further constraints: social and economic inferiority exacerbate an already handicapped ethnic minority. Our Khmer culture has left little place for women to grow and progress. The improvements in the standards of living all over the country, not only in urban areas, should hopefully contribute to this, and the presence of elected women in all political and social instances of the country must be a priority.

I often reread Michael Vickery's writings on the Khmer Rouge period in order to put it all in context. This is what he said concerning Region 41 where we were held: "All refugees from among the urban evacuees agree, either from experience or hearsay, that Damban 41, not far from Phnom Penh to the north east, was the worst of all, and that within that area, the district of Prey Chhor would take the prize for brutality[1]".

To get through it all, I often thought of the education of my parents whom I had frequently criticised. To nourish my internal resistance, I was inspired by my education to get through major hardships during that Khmer Rouge period. Like Vanny and Kim Touch, I survived by drawing the strength I needed to survive from my childhood and education, so I would live to see the Old and New people reunited in one Khmer identity. Vanny often talks of her *karma*, wondering what she must have done in past lives to have incurred such brutality. She seems relieved, however, considering the extraordinary luck she had to survive.

---

[1]   See *Cambodia 1975-1982*, South End Press, 1984, p. 123.

Executioners, surviving victims, or witnesses of past terror all carry within themselves the wound of history in various degrees. Many try to plunge into modern consumer society, while others remain on the side of the road, like the villagers of Phum Thmey. Each one does what he can to find a balance.

In the places that I visit again, people are enjoying their freedom, but they live in destitution and still bear the scars of history. Nothing has yet been done to really relieve them or to heal their trauma. The Khmer Rouge period remains in their memories like a badly-healed wound. They suffer from it as an amputee often suffers from a phantom limb. They avoid talking about a subject that is still taboo or forbidden.

In December 1978, after three years of attacks from the Khmer Rouge against its territory, "Vietnam invaded Democratic Kampuchea," according to the terms used by the Khmer Rouge in Cambodia. The world discovered the mass crimes hidden between 1975 and 1979, but the new People's Republic of Kampuchea wasn't recognised. The ambassador of Democratic Kampuchea sat in Cambodia's seat in the United Nations for another 14 years. Thus, the executioners were representing their victims, despite the fact that they were continuing to massacre people living in the zones they controlled. Westerners and the Chinese helped to reconstitute Pol Pot's army in Thailand.

In 1979, a "people's revolutionary tribunal" was set up to try the two leaders of Democratic Kampuchea, Pol Pot, "Brother Number One" and Ieng Sary, Deputy Prime Minister and Minister of Foreign Affairs. The new power didn't have sufficient military means to arrest them, and both were condemned to death in absentia. In June 1997, the Cambodian authorities asked for "the help of the United Nations to set up a special tribunal to try those who were responsible for genocide and crimes against humanity under the regime of Democratic Kampuchea". The United Nations suggested an international tribunal but Cambodia preferred a national court of law, helped by foreign magistrates.

The United Nations insisted that international legal criteria be respected, asked for guarantees concerning the arrest of suspects, and demanded the participation of foreign magistrates at all stages of the procedure. For the justice of my country, two problems arose: the Cambodian magistrates were all in one degree or another both judge and plaintiff and, furthermore, the Cambodian magistracy, which had been reconstituted after 1982, didn't have the training necessary to keep up with international standards. The solution of a mixed tribunal would allow the Cambodian magistracy to overcome these difficulties, and the presence of foreign magistrates was a guarantee of objectivity and of respect for the rights of both the defence and the victims.

In 2001, a law was passed leading to the creation of a competent tribunal destined to judge the leaders of the Khmer Rouge regime. It was set up at the heart of the Cambodian tribunals. The preliminary hearing, placed under the joint responsibility of the co-prosecutors and co-examining Cambodian and international magistrates, began in 2007. Following on from the terms of agreement between the Royal Government of Cambodia and the United Nations, the extraordinary courts will try the leaders of Democratic Kampuchea, plus the main people responsible for the serious crimes and violations of Cambodian criminal law and international humanitarian law—as well as the international agreements recognised by Cambodia—committed between 17 April 1975 and 6 January 1979. Today, at the end of 2007, five former leaders (Kaing Guek Eav alias Duch, Nuon Chea, Khieu Samphan, Ieng Sary, and Ieng Thirith) have been arrested and remanded in custody by the extraordinary courts. Pol Pot and Ta Mok both died without having been tried.

Such was the objective of this trial—a trial limited by the number of accused and highly ambitious from a judicial, historical, and political point of view—which opened in 2007, more than 30 years after the events in question. It seems too late to envisage a Truth and Reconciliation Commission, as in Argentina or South Africa, but it is never too late to try inalienable crimes which are beyond time limits, and even forgiveness. We are counting on justice, on our own justice with international support, to recognise the status of victims and make moral amends to them, by clarifying the responsibility of the perpetrators. We want all the dead to rest in peace and the survivors to find peace. But we eagerly await what is called the victims' "memorial truth". Only then will we be able to turn over a new leaf. Was it genocide, war crimes, or crimes against humanity? Only a judicial court will be able to provide that answer to the Cambodian people and the international community.

We owe this trial to the memory of the victims. We owe it to all of humanity to recognise genocide and reinforce the rule of law in our country. But the duty to remember doesn't stop there. It implies that this painful period must be integrated into our history, taught in our schools, and be the object of a true dialogue between the generations, so that this wound can finally be healed.

The Khmer are mostly Buddhists, even if the practice of Buddhism is often formal and superficial. We believe in *karma* which is the sum of our good or evil actions. No one can avoid the consequences of his actions, and this principle impregnates our culture and our dignity. We are the product of our actions, and this is what is hard for us to bear. Voluntary acts, whether positive or negative, in our speech, our thoughts, our feelings, or our physical actions, breed results. But that doesn't exclude justice or the collective rereading of history. Through *karma*, Buddhism liberates us from vengeance, which is good, but it doesn't liberate each of us from his own examination of conscience, from the duty to remember or, more broadly, from the initiative to remember. This latter task, which can occur through dialogue, but also through justice and law, has for too long been evaded, even though it alone will be able to cure our country of its past.

<u>The Angkor air</u>

Sadness in the evening sun
Flocks of kingfishers
Perch along streams.
Sadness in the evening sun,
While someone plays the air of Angkor,
A royal air, to put a king to sleep.
Sadness in the evening sun!
Here flocks of blackbirds
Sit at the top of the sdok tree.
But me and my love
Never catch each other's eye:
We watch the far horizons of our countries
Hers and mine.
As the sun sets I remove my turban
And walk along the forest's edge.
I walk and walk
My eyes look for her.
I walk along the forest's edge
And find my love drawing water
Under a hazy sky.

GLOSSARY OF VOCABULARY USED BY THE KHMER ROUGE, AND EVERYDAY WORDS

Achar: a specialist in ritual.

Angkar: the "Organisation" which governed all political and administrative levels in Democratic Kampuchea.

Angkar damban: an administrative region in Democratic Kampuchea.

Angkar pak-dek-vat: revolutionary organisation.

Auv: top part of a costume, shirt, or tunic.

Auv bam-porng: long tunic in the form of a tube.

Auv chen: Chinese tunic.

Auv kor-trorng: a traditional Khmer jacket.

Bay: rice cooked according to Khmer tradition.

Bay-dam-noeub-sang-kya: a dessert prepared with cooked glutinous rice, served with flan.

Boeung: a pond.

Borbor: rice soup with very little rice and lots of water. Poor people eat soup in the evening.

Borbor khap: thick rice soup.

Borbor reav: liquid rice soup.

Borng: older sister or older brother.

Chap-arom: marriage requested only by men and agreed in particular instances by the Angkar, who had the power to decide and organise the union between men and women.

Chhan: to eat. This term was unique to the bonzes.

Chhlôp: the Angkar militia, or spy-watch.

Chol Chhnam: Khmer New Year.

Chorng kben: tied with a kben.

Dak-kluon: to yield, a term used often during criticism and self-criticism meetings. Everyone had to yield to self-criticism and submit to criticism from the members of the meeting.

Dak-ruom: collective ownership of all private property, goods, and even human beings.

Dam-doeum-kor: "to plant the kapok tree" is a nice metaphor for to "close one's mouth", because the word *kor* in Khmer means "dumb" and in many circumstances it was better to keep one's mouth shut.

Dek: to sleep.

Guru: a guide with supernatural powers. Many gurus were spared by the various purges.

Haul: traditional Khmer patterned silk fabric.

Kabas: cotton plant.

Kam-chat: to eliminate

Kam-ma-sit-som-rom ballot muoy: a simple bundle, which contained the only personal objects we were allowed under Democratic Kahmpuchea.

Kam-tech: to demolish.

Kam-tech-van-nak: destruction of social classes.

Kar-than: a works project or site.

Khan Sla: gifts to the bride.

Khaur-chen: Chinese trousers.

Khlean: to be very hungry

Khos-sel-theur: to have sexual relations outside marriage.

Kmaing: enemy or traitor, a term used to describe someone who didn't obey the Organisation. Sooner or later he had to be eliminated. The word also described New people from 17 April 1975.

Korngchalat: a mobile section or front line brigade, generally made up of single people, which the Angkar sent around to all its major works projects.

Korngchalat chean-muk: the most productive *korngchalat*.

Korngchalat khlaing: the strongest *korngchalat*.

Korng-tauch: a sub-section of a *korngchalat* composed of 30 or 40 members.

Korng-thom: a section of the army of the *korngchalat* made up of 120-130 members.

Kor-sang-khluon: to forge oneself.

Krama: traditional multi-purpose scarf, in white and red squares, black and red, white and blue, white and green, etc. in cotton or silk. The *krama* is one of the indispensable pieces of clothing in daily Khmer life. It may be used as a scarf or rolled around the hips, to protect from the sun, to carry objects, to serve as a hammock for babies, or as a towel.

Krom sa-ma-ki: rural solidarity group formed in 1979 to replace the Khmer Rouge cooperatives.

Krousar: a family, husband, or wife according to terms introduced by the Khmer Rouge.

Kum-rou house: a model house built under the Democratic Kampuchean regime to accommodate the re-educated population.

Makleur: a wild fruit which is used to dye clothes black.

Meak-bo-chea: the festival of the Buddha.

Mia: uncle.

Mitt: comrade; the use of this word was imposed during the Khmer Rouge regime.

Neak-ta: protective earth spirits, masters of the water and land, dispensers of blessings. They were the object of a permanent religion until 1975.

Nham: to eat. This term is used more in well-off circles or with children.

Old and New people, 17 April people: see *Pror-chea*.

Pchum-ben: the festival in memory of the dead, in October of the lunar calendar.

Pdey and *pror-pourn*: husband and wife.

Pror-chea-chun-thmey: New people or the people of 17 April 1975 and, more precisely, New people from 1973 or 1975. This was an expression used to refer to the population liberated in 1973 and 1975 by the Angkar.

Pror-chea-chun-chas or *neak-moulthan*: Old people, an expression used to describe the population living in rural areas in the zones liberated by the Angkar before the victory of 17 April 1975.

Phlaunn: 40 units, a bunch of 40 rice plants, or 40 fruit.

Phteas-bay-ruom: communal kitchen or canteen under the regime of Democratic Kampuchea.

Pha-muong: traditional Khmer silk fabric without a pattern.

Pror-yut: to combat, the verb frequently used by the Khmer Rouge for all sorts of tasks.

Rieap-kar: the traditional expression for "to get married".

Rieap-krousar: to marry, a term introduced by the Khmer Rouge to describe the union of a man and a woman. The term is no longer used today.

Sam-pot-chorng-kben: a sampot tied at the back with a *kben*.

Sam-pot-sam-loy: a very simple *sampot* worn with or without a belt, tied at the front in the form of a knot at the waist, which the women wear practically every day.

Sam-rak: to rest; this word was more frequently used by the Khmer Rouge than the term "to sleep", which for them evoked laziness.

Sam-rok: to work relentlessly.

Sang-kum-reast-ni-yum: a working-class socialist society founded by Prince Norodom Sihanouk in 1955, which he continued to lead until the coup on 18 March 1970.

Sbauv: a wild plant used to make roofs for houses or for tying bunches of rice plants.

Sahakor: a basic cooperative created by the Angkar.

San-tek-sok: security force. The *San-tek-sok* played the role of political police and spy-watchers.

Sleak-peang-sleak-paaut OR *sleak-phteas*: to hide one's nakedness behind the house's earthenware jar.

Sras: pond or lake.

Sreut: neurovegetative illness common in the region of Kampong Cham. *Sreut* is the word used to describe all crises of tetany, often provoked by lack of calcium.

Ta: grandfather

Toeuk-doh-mday-thlay: a Khmer saying, which means, "My mother's milk is precious and protects me."

Toeuk-kbong: a sort of traditional Khmer detergent made from kapok leaves or dried banana skins, which are reduced to ashes then soaked for a night to produce a clear liquid to wash clothes and serve as soap.

Tum-nop-toeuk: a dam.

Vey-kan-dal: a married person.

Vi-sak-bo-chea: a Buddhist festival.

Vi-tiuk (pali): a more literary word for radio. In everyday life, the word "radio", borrowed from French, is more usual.

Wat or *Vat*: a pagoda or Buddhist monastery.

Yeay: grandmother.

Yothea: a Khmer Rouge soldier.

You-veak-neary: a young girl.

OVERVIEW OF THE ADMINISTRATIVE ORGANISATION OF
DEMOCRATIC KAMPUCHEA IN THE PROVINCES

THE ANGKAR

The Angkar means the "Organisation", that is to say the revolutionary organ of the Khmer Rouge which was the emanation of the CPK, the Communist Party of Kampuchea, and which would merge with it in 1977. In fact, the complete name is Angkar *padévat*, meaning the "Revolutionary Organisation". This was the central and local administration, governed by Pol Pot, whom we never saw at our humble level, but whose hold on power we felt sharply. This hold was applied through the Angkar *loeu*, which meant the "Superior Organisation", which grouped leaders at the summit of the hierarchy, located at the central committee of the CPK in Phnom Penh. For the then totally rural population, everything came back to the supreme and discretionary Angkar authority, which was in reality the behest of Pol Pot and the Central Committee.

Among civil servants, the cadres—in Khmer *ka-ma-phi-bal*—were the people close to power placed in the Angkar administration and in the army of Democratic Kampuchea, i.e. the Khmer Rouge. Cadre means the members of the political bureau of the party, the ministers, the high functionaries in the various ministries, zones, regions, districts, communes, or in the army. Under the regime of Democratic Kampuchea, civil servants were in symbiosis with soldiers. One couldn't distinguish between the two bodies, administrative functions being generally assigned to the military.

Ka-ma-phi-bal occupied various posts whose titles were often mentioned in relation to the supervisory staff, the members of the politburo, and ministers. These included the following:

- The *pror-thean phum-pheak* was chief of a zone, which was the biggest administrative division in Democratic Kampuchea. From 1975 onwards, the country was divided into seven different zones: centre, east, north, northeast, northwest, west, and southwest. The region where I was located was Region 41 of Preah Chhor, belonging to the centre zone, the only one not touching a border, which considerably reduced any possibility of escape. This zone, originally placed under the responsibility of Koy Thuon, who was eliminated for being too open to the value of education, was restructured in 1977[1] under the management of Ke Pauk.

- The *dambonn* was a regional chief. The zones were divided into *dam-born*, made up of 30 regions and two cities, Phnom Penh, and Sihanoukville.

---

1   See *Cambodia 1975-1982*, South End Press, 1984, p. 123.

- The *pror-thean srok* was head of the district. The *dam-born* were divided into *srok*. Each district was governed by two people the *pror-thean* and *anuk-pror-thean srok*, president and vice-president of the district.

- The chief of the basic economic unit, the *sahakor* cooperative which grouped several villages, was the *pror-thean sahakor*. The village population was placed at the disposition of the *sahakor*, which led agricultural activities from the time the land was pooled.

As well as those, several groupings completed the organisation of the population: *sama-kum you-veak-chun, sama-kum you-veak-nea-ry* and *sama-kum vey-kan-dal* which were youth associations of boys, girls, or married people.

THE KORNGCHALAT

The *korngchalat*, which means "mobile unit", was a grouping of single men and women over 16 years of age. Its members, divided into Old and New people, were part of the "first line force or brigade", the second brigade consisting of married people. They were sent to the hardest and most thankless works projects of the Angkar. The *korngchalat* was divided into *korng-vea-reak* of 360 people, themselves composed of three *korng-thom*. Each *korng-thom* of 120 had three *korng-tauch* of 40 people. Each *korng-tauch* was divided into three groups of between two and twelve people. The *korngchalat* was placed under the supervision of Angkar-appointed cadres. Each *korngchalat* unit was managed by a leader and one or more deputies.

Our *korng-vea-reak* of girls was made up of about 360 girls at its creation in 1975. The numbers didn't rise, but were rather reduced by the various purges and waves of missing persons.

Concerning justice, the Khmer Rouge completely wiped out the past, which was logical because the old judicial system was to them a tool for the domination and exploitation of the people. The Constitution of Democratic Kampuchea of 5 January 1976 enlightens us as to the initial intentions of the regime. Article 9 stipulates: "Justice is administered by people's tribunals which represent and defend the justice of the people, the democratic liberties of the people, and punish all actions carried out against the popular State or violating the laws of that state. The judges at all levels are chosen and nominated by the People's Representative Assembly".

The judiciary power, therefore, had its origins in working class representation, which conforms to communist regimes. But those principles were never put into practice. In fact, the people had no place, the people's representatives were never nominated, and we were never to see those courts function. For that to happen the Communist Party of Kampuchea would have had to want the emergence of a popular power of elected representatives, but a theoretical construct like this couldn't suit such a regime. What is more, a judiciary organisation would have necessitated educated cadres, and above all magistrates, clerks of court, and lawyers to defend victims and defendants. But these had all disappeared. By 1979, only three or four magistrates had survived in the whole country.

BIBLIOGRAPHY

BECKER Elisabeth: *When the war was over*, Public Affairs Books, 1986.

DY Kamboly: *A History of Democratic Kampuchea*, DCAM, 2007.

JENNAR Raoul M.: *Les Clés du Cambodge*, Maisonneuve & Larose, 1995.

KANE Solomon: *Dictionnaire des Khmers rouges*, Irasec, 2007.

KIERNAN Ben and CHANDLER D., *Aftermaths in Kampuchea*, Yale University, 1983.

LECLÈRE Adhémard: *Les Codes cambodgiens*, 1898.

LOCARD Henri: *Le Petit Livre rouge de Pol Pot*, L'Harmattan, 1996.

LUCO Fabienne, *Entre le tigre et le crocodile*, Unesco, 2002.

Ministère de Culture: *Phnom Penh, développement urbain et patrimoine*, 1990.

Ministère de Culture: *Phnom Penh, développement urbain et patrimoine*, 1993.

Ministère de l'Information du Gouvernement royal du Cambodge: *Cambodge*, 1962.

Népote Jacques: *Parenté et organisation sociale dans le Cambodge moderne et contemporain*, Oilizane, 1992.

Procheasas (Cambodian research group): *Cambodge. Population et société d'aujourd'hui*, L'Harmattan, 2005.

Siao-Ling Chow: *Volcan*, Acropoles, 1984.

Thierry Solange: *Les Khmers*, Kailash, 1996.

Thompson Ashley: *Le Rappel des âmes*, texte rituel khmer, éditions Reyum, 2001.

Vickery Michael: *Cambodia 1975-1982*, South End Press, 1984.

CONSTITUTION OF DEMOCRATIC KAMPUCHEA
5 JANUARY 1976

PREAMBLE

On the basis of the sacred and fundamental desires of the people, workers, peasants, and other labourers as well as those of the fighters and cadres of the Kampuchean Revolutionary Army; and

Whereas a significant role has been played by the people, especially the workers, poor peasants, the lower middle peasantry, and other strata of labourers in the countryside and cities, who account for more than ninety-five percent of the entire Kampuchean nation, who assumed the heaviest responsibility in waging the war for the liberation of the nation and the people, made the greatest sacrifices in terms of life, property, and commitment, served the front line relentlessly, and unhesitatingly sacrificed their children and husbands by the thousands for the fight on the battlefield;

Whereas great sacrifices have been borne by the three categories of the Kampuchean Revolutionary Army who fought valiantly, day and night, in the dry and rainy season, underwent all sorts of hardship and misery, shortages of food, medicine, clothing, ammunition, and other commodities in the great war for the liberation of the nation and the people;

Whereas the entire Kampuchean people and the entire Kampuchean Revolutionary Army desire an independent, unified, peaceful, neutral, non-aligned, sovereign Kampuchea enjoying territorial integrity, a national society informed by genuine happiness, equality, justice, and democracy without rich or poor and without exploiters or exploited, a society in which all live harmoniously in great national solidarity and join forces to do manual labour together and increase production for the construction and defence of the country;

And whereas the resolution of the Special National Congress held on 25, 26 and 27 April 1975 solemnly proclaimed recognition and respect for the above desires of the entire people and the entire Kampuchean Revolutionary Army;

The Constitution of Kampuchea states:

CHAPTER ONE
The State

Article 1 The State of Kampuchea is an independent, unified, peaceful, neutral, non-aligned, sovereign, and democratic State enjoying territorial integrity.

The State of Kampuchea is a State of the people, workers, peasants, and all other Kampuchean labourers.

The official name of the State of Kampuchea is "Democratic Kampuchea".

CHAPTER TWO
The Economy

Article 2 All important general means of production are the collective property of the people's State and the common property of the people's collectives.

Property for everyday use remains in private hands.

CHAPTER THREE
Culture

Article 3 The culture of Democratic Kampuchea has a national, popular, forward-looking, and healthful character such as will serve the tasks of defending and building Kampuchea into an ever more prosperous country.

This new culture is absolutely opposed to the corrupt, reactionary culture of the various oppressive classes and that of colonialism and imperialism in Kampuchea.

CHAPTER FOUR
The Principle of Leadership and Work

Article 4 Democratic Kampuchea applies the collective principle in leadership and work.

CHAPTER FIVE
Legislative Power

Article 5 Legislative power is invested in the representative assembly of the people, workers, peasants, and all other Kampuchean labourers.

This Assembly shall be officially known as the "Kampuchean People's Representative Assembly".

The Kampuchean People's Representative Assembly shall be made up of 250 members, representing the people, the workers, peasants, and all other Kampuchean labourers and the Kampuchean Revolutionary Army. Of these 250, there shall be:

- Representing the peasants 150
- Representing the labourers and other working people 50
- Representing the revolutionary army 50

Article 6 The members of the Kampuchean People's Representative Assembly are to be elected by the people through direct and prompt general elections by secret ballot to be held throughout the country every five years.

Article 7 The People's Representative Assembly is responsible for legislation and for defining the various domestic and foreign policies of Democratic Kampuchea.

CHAPTER SIX
The Executive Body

Article 8 The administration is a body responsible for executing the laws and political lines of the Kampuchean People's Representative Assembly.

The administration is elected by the Kampuchean People's Representative Assembly and must be fully responsible to the Kampuchean People's Representative Assembly for all its activities inside and outside the country.

CHAPTER SEVEN
Justice

Article 9 Justice is administered by people's courts, representing and defending the people's justice, defending the democratic rights and liberties of the people, and condemning any activities directed against the people's State or violating the laws of the people's State.

The judges at all levels will be chosen and appointed by the People's Representative Assembly.

Article 10 Actions violating the laws of the people's State are as follows:

Dangerous activities in opposition to the people's State must be condemned to the highest degree.

Other cases are subject to constructive re-education in the framework of the State's or people's organisations.

CHAPTER EIGHT
The State Presidium

Article 11 Democratic Kampuchea has a State Presidium chosen and appointed by the Kampuchean People's Representative Assembly once every five years.

The State Presidium is responsible for representing the State of Democratic Kampuchea inside and outside the country in keeping with the Constitution of Democratic Kampuchea and with the laws and political lines of the Kampuchean People's Representative Assembly.

The State Presidium is composed as follows: a president, a first vice-president, and a second vice-president.

CHAPTER NINE
The Rights and Duties of the Individual

Article 12 Every citizen of Kampuchea enjoys full rights to a constantly improving material, spiritual, and cultural life.

Every citizen of Democratic Kampuchea is guaranteed a living.
All workers are the masters of their factories.
All peasants are the masters of the rice paddies and fields.
All other labourers have the right to work.
There is absolutely no unemployment in Democratic Kampuchea.

Article 13 There must be complete equality among all Kampuchean people in an equal, just, democratic, harmonious, and happy society within the great national solidarity for defending and building the country together.

Men and women are fully equal in every respect.
Polygamy is prohibited.

Article 14 It is the duty of all to defend and build the country together in accordance with individual ability and potential.

CHAPTER TEN
The Capital

Article 15 The capital city of Democratic Kampuchea is Phnom Penh.

CHAPTER ELEVEN
The National Flag

Article 16 The design and significance of the Kampuchean national flag are as follows:

The background is red, with a yellow three-towered temple in the middle.

The red background symbolises the revolutionary movement, the resolute and valiant struggle of the Kampuchean people for the liberation, defence, and construction of their country.

The yellow temple symbolises the national traditions of the Kampuchean people, who are defending and building the country to make it ever more prosperous.

CHAPTER TWELVE
The National Emblem

Article 17 The national emblem consists of a network of dikes and canals, which symbolise modern agriculture, and factories, which symbolise industry. These are framed by an oval garland of rice ears, with the inscription "Democratic Kampuchea" at the bottom.

CHAPTER THIRTEEN
The National Anthem

Article 18 The national anthem of Democratic Kampuchea is the "*Dap Prampi Mesa Chokchey*" ["Glorious Seventeenth of April"].

CHAPTER FOURTEEN
The Kampuchean Revolutionary Army

Article 19 The three categories of the Kampuchean Revolutionary Army—regular, regional, and guerrilla—form an army of the people made up of men and women fighters and cadres who are the children of the labourers, peasants, and other Kampuchean working people. They defend the State power of the Kampuchean people and of independent, unified, peaceful, neutral, non-aligned, sovereign, and democratic Kampuchea, which enjoys territorial integrity, and at the same time they help to build a country growing more prosperous every day to improve and develop the people's standard of living.

CHAPTER FIFTEEN
Worship and Religion

Article 20 Every citizen of Kampuchea has the right to worship according to any religion and the right not to worship according to any religion.

Reactionary religions which are detrimental to Democratic Kampuchea and Kampuchean people are absolutely forbidden.

CHAPTER SIXTEEN
Foreign Policy

Article 21 Democratic Kampuchea fervently and earnestly desires to maintain close and friendly relations with all countries sharing a common border and with all those near and distant throughout the world in conformity with the principles of mutual and absolute respect for sovereignty and territorial integrity.

Democratic Kampuchea adheres to a policy of independence, peace, neutrality and non-alignment. It will permit absolutely no foreign country to maintain military bases on its territory and is resolutely opposed to all forms of outside interference in its internal affairs, and to all forms of subversion and aggression against Democratic Kampuchea from outside, whether military, political, cultural, social, diplomatic, or humanitarian.

Democratic Kampuchea refuses all intervention in the domestic affairs of other countries, and scrupulously respects the principle that every country is sovereign and entitled to manage and decide its own affairs without outside interference.

Democratic Kampuchea remains absolutely within the great family of non-aligned nations.

Democratic Kampuchea strives to promote solidarity with the peoples of the Third World in Asia, Africa, and Latin America, and with peace- and justice-loving people the world over, and to contribute most actively to mutual aid and support in the struggle against imperialism, colonialism, neo-colonialism, and in favour of independence, peace, friendship, democracy, justice, and progress in the world.

Adopted by the Third National Congress on 14 December 1975 and brought into force on 5 January 1976.